RICHARD KIRK

LESSONS FROM HEAVEN

outskirts press

Timmy's Wish
Lessons From Heaven
All Rights Reserved.
Copyright © 2024 Richard Kirk
v2.0

The opinions expressed in this manuscript are solely the opinions of the author and do not represent the opinions or thoughts of the publisher. The author has represented and warranted full ownership and/or legal right to publish all the materials in this book.

This book may not be reproduced, transmitted, or stored in whole or in part by any means, including graphic, electronic, or mechanical without the express written consent of the publisher except in the case of brief quotations embodied in critical articles and reviews.

Outskirts Press, Inc.
http://www.outskirtspress.com

Paperback ISBN: 978-1-9772-7087-0
Hardback ISBN: 978-1-9772-7088-7

Cover Photo © 2024 www.gettyimages.com. All rights reserved - used with permission.

Outskirts Press and the "OP" logo are trademarks belonging to Outskirts Press, Inc.

PRINTED IN THE UNITED STATES OF AMERICA

Dedication
TO MOM, DAD, COLEEN,
AND OF COURSE,
TIMMY

TABLE OF CONTENTS

INTRODUCTION I
Chapter 1: THE FAMILY 1
Chapter 2: TIMMY'S WISH 10
Chapter 3: THE NEWS 17
Chapter 4: AN ARDUOUS JOURNEY BEGINS 21
Chapter 5: A CROWN OF THORNS 28
Chapter 6: A BOY ON A MISSION 34
Chapter 7: HAIL MARY 42
Chapter 8: I WISH I WERE A CHURCH 47
Chapter 9: AND I WOULD JOIN THEM IN PRAYER 55
Chapter 10: THE BREAKDOWN 59
Chapter 11: A DAY AT THE BEACH 67
Chapter 12: REUNITED 74
Chapter 13: THE WAY FORWARD 80
Chapter 14: HEALING INVOLVES ACTION 86
EPILOGUE 97
CHAPTER NOTES 101
ACKNOWLEDGEMENTS 104

INTRODUCTION

Every life is a lesson. This is a phrase that has stuck with me over the years, although I cannot recall its origin. But it is a suggestion to us that every life carries a message that provides opportunities to learn from their achievements or their transgressions, their choices, and the resulting consequences. We study the lives of saints and sinners, heroes and villains to try to glean some subtle or not-so-subtle lessons that we can use to guide us in our actions. An entire business model has developed around the individuals whose fall from grace and subsequent rise from the ashes of poor decision-making are somehow supposed to be a model for the rest of us. The "don't be like me" industry has no shortage of employees.

But we shouldn't have to look very far to find our saints and heroes. In many cases, they are with us every day and are an integral part of our lives. They are authentic and they have made the right choices all along. They have worked hard, prayed hard, and sacrificed often. They have clothed us, fed us, held our hand when we needed comfort, picked us up when we have fallen, and accepted us for who we are while inspiring us to be the best versions of ourselves. They have reminded us, time and time again, that we matter and what we do and what we say matter. They taught us lessons in faith, family, friendship, accountability, responsibility, and service. These are the lessons we have learned from our parents, grandparents, siblings, friends, teachers, and coaches, and we consolidate them into a framework for our own lives.

We make decisions based on those values to construct a path to a purposeful life. In charting that path, we try to practice the best qualities of the champions in life and hopefully avoid the pitfalls afflicting the fallen angels so we can fulfill the hopes and dreams we all have and that our families have had for us.

Some lives, however, are unique. They stand out from the ordinary. They provide a masterclass of hope and inspiration. Whether they are first responders who protect and serve their communities, the veterans who swore to give up their lives for their country, the missionaries who travel to the poorest regions of the world to selflessly provide lifesaving care to the hungry and diseased, or the survivors of catastrophic illnesses or injuries who overcome their conditions to accomplish incredible feats, they transcend the norm and challenge us to be exceptional if we are willing to learn from them. Their stories provide us with the direction we need on the journey that makes us human, the journey to a purposeful and impactful life.

I am blessed to have been able to learn from so many wonderful individuals. My parents, my sister, teachers, coaches, friends, and clergy have provided examples of how to navigate the successes and failures that contribute to a life experience with humility and integrity. Yet, what I have come to understand and appreciate is that the most profound influence on my journey has been the life of my younger brother, Timmy, the subject of this book.

This is the book my father wanted to write but never seemed to be able to summon the strength and courage to relive the years that challenged his resolve, his patience, his purpose, and his faith. He felt Timmy's story was important enough to share, not only for who he was but how he lived his life and inspired others. My father did not want to see Timmy's story die with him. He had mentioned several times that he wanted to write a book, but it was clear that the task was going to take him to a place where he would be forced to confront the pain and suffering of not only his son but his own. I don't blame him for letting the clock run out on this one.

Toward the end of his life, he asked if I would want to write a book about my brother. I would do anything for my father, but this was going to be a heavy lift. I told him I would consider it and left it at that. Not only is writing a book a rigorous task requiring significant focus and energy but writing one so personal added to the challenge. Like my father, I was not sure I had the courage to go there. Being a private individual, it is difficult to share such intimate experiences, and it was necessary to get past that obstacle to take on this project. In the few years after my father's passing, the thought of writing a book, any book, much less one so personal, stayed with me. I felt I owed it to my father to at least try. He was right to think it was a story that should be told, yet I had reservations about my ability to do it justice.

Despite being a deeply personal account of a boy, his family, and their journey of faith, this book is a testament to the impact that one life can have on so many, along with lessons of courage, hope, and the search for purpose and meaning in life. With my father's blessing and my eternal respect for his courage and for the lessons he and my mother have provided us, I will humbly attempt to bring the message of Timmy's journey to light. This is a story of his Wish, his faith, his purpose, and the lessons that he has imparted to us along the way and continues to provide to this day. It is the story of a boy whose faith was as foundational as his life was tragic. It is a story of a family's journey of hope and resilience while confronting the fear and doubt that come with the inevitable cruelties of life's reality, in this case, the ravages of childhood cancer. It is a story experienced through my eyes and in my heart as I have lived it, challenging me to confront my mortality and shortcomings while searching for a purpose of my own.

I am very aware that time and distance undoubtedly play tricks with one's memories. There are events and circumstances in this true account that are forever seared into my mind with such clarity, it's as if they happened only yesterday, and they still trigger the same feelings and emotions as they did before. Other memories required a little more coaxing and verifying along the way to ensure the events were properly detailed and sequenced by way of evidence or supported by the contributions of others, but included as they were vital to the context of the story. Some details are more essential than others, and those were the ones I included and dutifully set out to memorialize accurately. As a result, this is a true story with true events about real people.

My parents have since passed on, and their contributions to this book would have been so informative and profoundly enriching in ways that I could never imagine. One of my regrets was that I failed to sit down with them and ask all the questions that have haunted me over the years. I was always reluctant to have them relive what was the most trying of times. I'm not sure if I was protecting them or myself. Being a traditional Irish family, we did not discuss difficult or emotional topics very often. If I knew there was a book to be written, I certainly would have made more of an effort to do so. I did have one or two opportunities to discuss some details with my father during my visits with him when he was hospitalized with one of the many ailments that he dealt with over the final years of his life, and I have included those in this book.

With apologies to the readers for any gaps that I could not reconcile, I did my best to accurately portray the moments, events, feelings, trials, and tribulations of a boy, his family, his journey, and his legacy. Any errors are mine and mine alone, and I have confidence they will not deter from the spirit and message that are being portrayed.

Another goal of this book is to shed some light on the traumatic effects of childhood tragedies and how they impact family members who care for their loved ones during diagnosis and treatment. Although Timmy was an exceptional individual, his story of suffering is not all that uncommon to those who are victims of pediatric cancer. The afflicted are cared for through the heroic work and dedication of doctors and nurses, the miracles of advanced medical care, and the thoughts, prayers, and generous donations of a community of caring supporters. However, the families involved will experience life-altering emotional, physical, and often financial burdens that they will undoubtedly shoulder for the rest of their lives. These families often suffer in silence as they try to piece together some explanation as to why this had to happen to their loved ones and find some elusive peace. Long after the momentum of support wanes and the cards and letters of sympathy stop coming, there is the inevitable challenge of dealing with grief and the relentless reminders of the indiscriminate reality of life itself. The family has their own story to tell.

One positive result that could come from the reading of this book would be that the experiences described here bring a sense of communion among the family, friends, and loved ones facing similar challenges who otherwise may feel alone and isolated as they cope with life-changing events. You are not alone, and there is help. Near the end of this book, I provide names of just some of the institutions that provide medical care for cancer patients along with extensive support care for families, organizations that raise funds for research, family outreach programs, and some ways you can help those who are experiencing loss.

Despite the suffering and sadness, *Timmy's Wish* is a lesson of profound inspiration. The lessons that I have learned have provided guidance as I continue to address the fundamental questions of my life and have helped me to discover my purpose. I hope that by reading this book, you can find commonality with the struggle and inspiration from his Wish, and discover the lessons that will help you realize your purpose and find peace along the way.

Chapter 1

THE FAMILY

Family—and the strength and support it provides—has always been an important priority throughout our lives. To truly appreciate Timmy's Wish is to understand the family who raised him and stood by his side. Being the third child in a typical middle-class family provided Timmy with the support and foundational, spiritual resources to realize his Wish and his purpose on Earth.

My parents were not very different from many of their generation. Growing up in circumstances with limited resources at best, they developed their worldview through the experiences of the Depression, World War II, Catholic doctrine, and adherence to family and community values.

My father, Eugene, was born in 1931 in Brooklyn, New York, during the height of the Great Depression, to a Jewish mother, Anna Seedner, and a Roman Catholic father, Michael Kirk. He was the youngest son in a family of eight other brothers and sisters all raised Roman Catholic. He was introduced to struggle right from the start.

The family lived in a three-room, railroad-style apartment that somehow housed ten people who shared a common hallway bathroom with other families on the floor. His father eked out a living as a butcher to support his growing family and sometimes, if they were lucky, would bring home scraps of meat cuttings from the shop that were to be discarded if they were not sold. His mother would find a creative way to turn these scraps into delicious meals that my father would later remember with fondness. He learned the lessons of humility and love of family through their struggles in mid-twentieth-century Brooklyn.

My father was an intelligent and curious student who had a desire to go to college and maybe even medical school. He was an avid reader and a deep thinker, and he possessed an effectively sarcastic sense of humor that endeared him to many of our family and friends. But like many young men of his generation, circumstances intervened. Shortly after high school, he enlisted in the army and was subsequently sent to Korea to serve his military obligation, rising to the level of Sergeant First Class while earning, among other citations, the Bronze Star and Distinguished Service medals.

Though he rarely talked about his experience, like many who have served in the armed forces, it had a profound impact on his perspective of the world. He was witness to some of the most horrific examples of human slaughter that war could provide. The idea of the inevitable mortality of life was not far from his thoughts.

My mother, Maureen, was born in 1935 in South Amboy, New Jersey, and was also raised Roman Catholic. Quiet and faithful, she lived her life with a strong belief in God and unwavering loyalty to family and friends. As with my father, she could not escape the heartlessness of life's malice. My mother was twelve when her mother died due to the effects of alcoholism, leaving my mother and her older sister, Nancy, to be raised by my grandfather, Edward Sullivan, the only grandparent I have ever known. His ability to properly care for his two young daughters was certainly compromised, and as a result, my mother and Nancy were to split time between New York and South Amboy, where they lived with an aunt and uncle while my grandfather lived and worked in Queens, New York. This is how they spent a portion of their formative years. Nancy eventually entered the convent as Sister Mary Catherine Sullivan, and my mother graduated from high school in Queens.

My mother entered the workforce, eventually taking a job at the headquarters of the *New York Daily News* in New York City. In her time at the *News*, she entered and won a company-sponsored beauty contest and was crowned Miss Page One. This award caught the attention of another employee of the *News*, Eugene Kirk, and fate intervened. Based on my mother's account, he invited himself to take her to the Miss Page One Ball celebration, and the rest was history. They became a couple and were married in 1957, started their own family while residing in the Woodside section of Queens, and began to pursue their version of the American Dream.

My sister, Coleen, was born in 1958, I followed in 1959, and Timothy arrived in 1963. My mother was devoted to her faith, doted on her children, and was a model of decency and kindness and well respected by all. She had a remarkable inner strength. This was to serve her well in the years ahead.

Faith was foundational in our family. My parents were devoted Catholics and instilled that culture in us. We attended church weekly, and many of our social and family gatherings centered around baptisms, first communions, confirmations, weddings, and birthdays as our extended family of aunts, uncles, cousins, nieces, and nephews provided a seemingly unending parade of celebrations.

4 ★ *Timmy's Wish*

Timmy, me, and Coleen mid-1960s Queens, NY

With a desire to own a house and move on from our small apartment and a crowded city, my parents made the move from Queens, New York, leaving behind family and friends and bringing their traditional values and optimistic outlook to Metuchen, New Jersey, a small working-class town about forty-five minutes outside of the city. They purchased a modest home on West Chestnut Avenue that although small came with an enclosed front porch, a basement, and a long driveway for my father's 1960s-era pale green Rambler. This is a big deal if all you know is apartment living. With a growing family, newly acquired friends, and that front porch, my parents' American Dream was being realized.

The house on West Chestnut Avenue, Metuchen 1966

My sister and I enrolled in the nearby St Francis of Assisi Grammar School overseen by the local parish and the Diocese of Trenton. The network of parish priests, Sisters of Mercy, Brothers of the Sacred Heart, and a collection of devoted lay teachers ran the school in the typically strict Catholic tradition. Since my aunt was a nun, we arrived already known to some of the good Sisters of the school. It was like an extended family.

That community offered a sense of comfort in one way and yet oddly annoying in another. The additional inhibitory effect on your behavior had a purpose. You couldn't get away with anything. Whatever you did, said, or even thought, they seemed to know about it. They knew your family, your neighbors, and your friends. Eyes seemed everywhere long before the era of electronic surveillance yet remarkably effective. If you found yourself in trouble, your parents knew about it before you arrived home and you could expect consequences to be handed down. There was no code of silence.

The Catholic community was close-knit. Neighbors became best friends and your second family. Everyone had shared life experiences stemming from humble beginnings. Many of the men had served in the armed forces during WWII or Korea. We saw each other in church each week and enjoyed block parties during the summer. Many of the adults belonged to the Knights of Columbus, a Catholic organization where community service alternated with holiday celebrations and help or assistance was always just a phone call away. When something happened in one family, it happened to everyone's family. It was all we knew, and we were to find out how important that was going forward.

My sister, Coleen, was the oldest child and duly suited for that role. Everything that we were to experience in childhood and as young adults, she was the first in line. I learned from her how to handle high school, driving lessons, college, and social life. I was to learn from her in the future about how to manage some of the biggest challenges in our lives. Though she was only about a year older, the difference in our level of emotional intelligence was stark.

Coleen was (and is) mature and rational, and she possesses a strong sense of duty and work ethic. She has my father's wisdom and my mother's compassion. She remains to this day a voice of reason and a source of strength both for me and her own family. Someone had to be the adult in the room when circumstances called for one, and she filled that role superbly.

I was the temperamental opposite. I was competitive, a little intense at times, and had a bit of a temper. I loved playing sports, especially baseball and basketball. It was not unusual for me to get into the occasional neighborhood scuffle over seemingly innocuous circumstances during local pickup games.

I loved to read and would often avail myself of the many books my father had shelved around the house. There were books about medicine and health, biographies, novels, current events, and horror. There were classics ranging from the writings of St. Thomas Aquinas to the secrets of the Vatican and Aesop's Fables. We even had a complete set of the Encyclopedia Americana, which we used often during school years for homework or other assignments. My growing interest was in the field of science. It was fascinating to learn about nature, the world, and the universe, and to this day these topics form much of my personal book collection. I enjoyed learning and liked to ask questions and challenge the prevailing wisdom. We were expected to go to college, not only for the educational and career advantages, but it was important to my parents, who were both very intelligent but never had that opportunity when they were young.

While we as a family followed the rules, rituals, and expectations of the Catholic traditions, I had questions about the necessity of some of these requirements. More directly, because of the irreverence of youthful skepticism, I thought they were ridiculous. Being the curious irritant that I was, I think it's fair to say I was not fond of being inconvenienced, and I felt the need to ask these essentially important questions.

"So why can't we eat meat on Friday during Lent? What's going to happen if I do?"

"Do I really have to give up something for Lent? Maybe I'll give up asking questions. Does that count?"

"Why can't I eat breakfast before 10:45 Sunday Mass? You expect me to not eat anything till noontime? What if I pass out in church? How would that look?"

"Why do the homilies have to be so long? Don't they know that half the people are falling asleep?"

During Mass, especially during those homilies, I would reflexively begin to daydream about my next game or activity as soon as the priest broke into his scintillating introduction, "In today's Gospel...zzzzz." My faith was not the problem. I just was not good with rules that made little sense to me.

My mother was less than thrilled that I would question the purpose of these long-standing traditions and would try to explain how sacrifice and compliance were part of being a good Catholic. Since I was rarely satisfied with that line of thought, it ultimately came down to the usual parental default line: "Because I said so." I would then appeal to my father, who I felt would be more understanding, only to be hit with another standard parental shutdown line: "Do what your mother says," he'd say as he looked at me with a detectable level of sympathy since I knew he felt breakfast was not a totally unreasonable request. Never receiving adequate answers to these questions, I did eventually acquiesce to the inconvenience of it all if I was going to live happily in this house by trying to be a good Catholic, even if I was only just an okay Catholic.

Timmy was four years old when we moved to New Jersey. He was the most dynamic presence in the family. He had a personality that could dominate the room and often did. He loved to tell jokes, perform impressions of comedic personalities who were on TV. He could air guitar to his favorite Beatles songs long before it was a thing and had an uncanny ability to captivate adults in his presence as he entertained them at family holiday gatherings. He didn't seem to have many friends his age, but that did not bother him. He preferred being around adults who became his adoring audience, and he enjoyed the feedback it provided. I could never understand how he was able to attract that sort of attention. It was surely not an ability the rest of us possessed. He certainly had a gift.

When in school Timmy had the strict but amiable nuns in his hip pocket as it were. He was clever, funny, and unusually religious for his age, and the nuns were impressed with his communication skills and sense of humor. He could make even the most stoic sister crack a smile. He had the "it" factor, whatever that is. Maybe the good sisters knew something we didn't.

In an ordinary town, in an ordinary family, Timmy was the extraordinary exception. He was the outlier. He was good-looking, charismatic, laugh-out-loud funny, and keenly intelligent. He had an unusual devotion to God and his Catholic faith. He had his copy of the Children's Bible, which he brought to Mass each week, and memorized all the stories. Most importantly, he had a purpose.

I have many positive and pleasant memories of those times in Metuchen. Who wouldn't? Life was simple and predictable. We were a happy, small-town family. We had friends, we had faith, and we had each other. We didn't have much, but we had what we needed, and that was more than okay.

Chapter 2

TIMMY'S WISH

Metuchen was a wonderful town in which to raise a family. You could walk or ride a bike anywhere. A little over 2.5 square miles, it has the feel of a mid-century Norman Rockwell reflection of Americana complete with a quaint downtown center on Main Street that would be home to parades and community celebrations offering the usual collection of hardware, shoe, and clothing stores and a pharmacy. Just past the southeast end of the downtown area of Main Street is the New Jersey Transit railroad line, which runs northeast and southwest, splitting the town in half. There are churches representing multiple denominations, a synagogue, a public library, Little League fields, a municipal pool for pretend summer vacations, a public elementary, middle, and high school, a Catholic elementary school, and a CYO (Catholic Youth Organization) building that housed a gymnasium in the shadows of the grand St. Francis Church, now since designated a cathedral.

The St. Francis Cathedral is undoubtedly the architectural centerpiece of the residential community. It towers over all other buildings and dwellings in the vicinity. For us children, it was an imposing presence proudly displaying an impressive circular stained glass window hovering over a decorative statue of St. Francis himself. The exterior is constructed of light gray mica-flecked granite stone, held in a cement framework, a large platform also of granite separating two levels of stairs leading to three front entrances each guarded by large, wooden, double doors opening to a foyer that leads into the church's center hall. Inside are row after row of wooden pews that can easily hold several hundred parishioners. The side walls of the church interior are covered in squares of marble up to about ten feet and above which is a line of seven brightly colored stained glass windows down each side. Extending from the midline and buttressing the ceiling are massive wooden beams that curve down the side walls to the floor. The marble altar stands humbly in the center of the sanctuary as a sentinel guarding the sacristy.

Seeing the cathedral today, it may not feel as imposing, but when we were young, it reminded us of how very small we are in the grand scheme of God's universe. It was a very impressive sight and certainly reflected the majesty of a cathedral. It is in these pews that we heard Mass, sang hymns, received the sacraments, and reflected on our sins before the occasional confession.

Not one for extensive confessional reflection, I can honestly say that my list of sins became somewhat, and conveniently, repetitive as I never felt comfortable entering the confessional without something to say even if I didn't feel I committed a sin that week. It just didn't seem right. I gave the priest a recycled list of general transgressions, received the standard issue of Our Fathers and Hail Marys, and hoped he didn't notice.

I never felt I was being dishonest with the priest since I did what I said I did at one time or another. Even having been absolved of them already, I couldn't go into the confessional and say, 'Bless me father, I had a good week, nothing to share today." I'm sure my penance would have kept me in the pew for hours.

St. Francis Catheral. Timmy's church

Coming from the quintessential Catholic family, and notwithstanding my prior lack of judgement, I served as an altar boy at St. Francis up to my eighth grade year. This extended the lineage of altar servers in the family as my father served in his church when he was young. I felt it was expected from my family but not required. Despite my aversion to and growing skepticism of certain arbitrary rules, I didn't mind serving as it made me feel part of the community and the CYO organization that came with it.

The priests were kind and professional. If you made the occasional mistake, such as forgetting to ring the bells during the consecration—a pretty big mistake, by the way, since this was the most sacred part of the Mass—a slight turn of the head and a nod would send the message. After Mass, a quick review of the cues and a discussion of teamwork between the servers was all that was required to get us back on track.

I imagine Timmy felt the same sense of grandeur in the presence of this impressive structure, which may have led him to contemplate the vast nature of it all and how he wanted to be part of this community of faith. To him, the church was more than a granite façade with marble floors and pretty windows. This was not what most children would be thinking. But he was not like most children.

In 1973, at the age of nine, Timmy was in the fourth grade at St. Francis. The class was issued an assignment that would be titled "My Wish." This was a common writing task that asked young students to express their thoughts and was reminiscent of other assignments such as: "What do you want to be when you grow up?" or some other prompt to practice their writing skills. Anyone who has ever been an elementary schoolteacher knows that student writing can certainly be entertaining and revealing. The simplicity exposes the thoughts of children searching to find the right words and phrases to express themselves. Many students of this age wish to be a firefighter, a sports hero, a teacher, a doctor, maybe wish for world peace, a million dollars, or a lifetime supply of ice cream that they may or may not share with friends.

As was his nature, Timmy took a different path. Faith was an important component of our family life, but it seemed to occupy more of my brother's thoughts than we realized. He was not one to openly verbalize or evangelize about his faith. However, it became clear that he thought deeply and developed a personal relationship with the faith. Even before he could read proficiently, he would page through the pictures of his Children's Bible as he learned all the stories he would eventually hear about in the sermons. The ease with which he interacted with priests and nuns was somewhat unusual for his age.

14 ★ *Timmy's Wish*

Timmy, age nine, around the time he wrote his Wish.

He enjoyed attending mass, singing hymns to which he knew all the words, and was comfortable in this domain. If there was anyone who would consider the priesthood as his vocation, it would be Timmy, and it would not have surprised anybody. But that is not what he wrote about. He was not content with the notion of a pedestrian parish priesthood. He was nine years old, and he had higher ambitions.

His teacher found his paper stuffed in his desk for some reason, but upon reading it, she was so taken by his writing that she shared it with my parents. I recall my mother telling me that the teacher had never read anything like this before. We found out that word had spread throughout the school staff about his paper. My parents shared it with our closest neighbors and then eventually enclosed it in a standard light brown wooden frame and hung it proudly on the dining room wall, where it remained until my father sold the house decades later.

I have walked through the dining room countless times glancing at it or stopping to read it in full, trying to figure out what he was trying to say. I was always curious as to how someone of his age came up with such a deeply complex idea while completing a writing assignment in class. Reading it served not only as a reminder of him but also of the power of the gift of purpose in one's life. It summarizes who he was and what he hoped to be. I was sure that most fourth graders do not write passages like this, so why him? Written in pencil on standard lined paper in rudimentary cursive penmanship, it reads:

My Wish

I wish I were a church and if I were, I would sit on the ground watching the people going into me. And I would join them in prayer. I'd be very special through out the whole town, because I'd ring my bell every hour.
Then I would be a house of God, to the end of the world.

—Timothy Kirk, February 1, 1973

It was brief and very powerful. This was not the expression of a typical nine-year-old boy. He was not just expressing his desire to serve the community as a priest or hoping for peace and goodwill throughout the land. He was at one with an institution and a faith. He had a higher calling. I certainly could not understand what he meant at the time. Maybe I wasn't supposed to—yet. While I had delusions of being a centerfielder for the New York Yankees, he dreamed of being the centerpiece of a community of faith and a beacon of hope for all who believed. I was beginning to realize that he was not like the rest of us. He had his own plan.

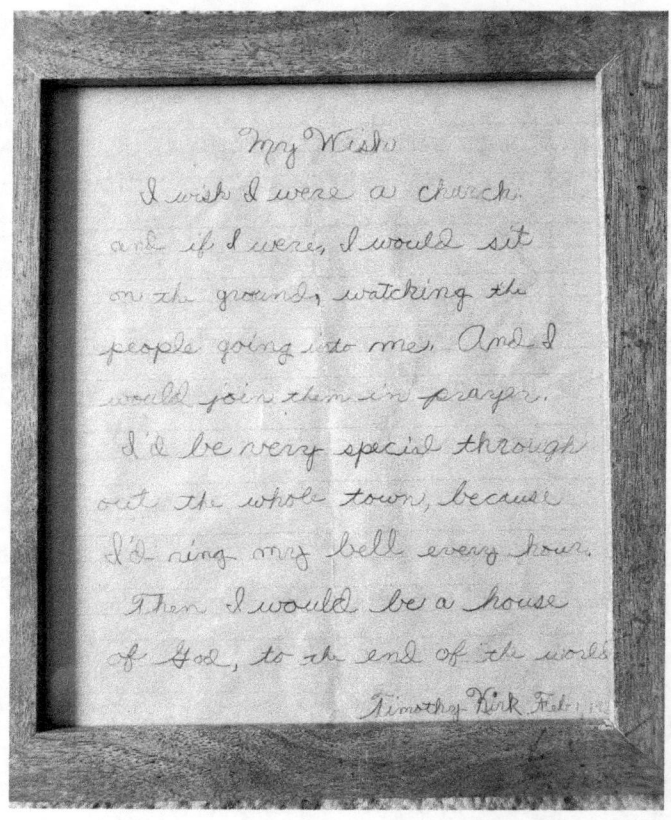

My Wish

Chapter 3

THE NEWS

Mom and Dad worked hard to make sure we had everything we needed. We never lacked the essentials of clothing and food. They supported our endeavors, which ranged from dancing and music lessons to Little League baseball. All our birthdays were celebrated with the enthusiasm that marked the uniqueness of each of us. Holidays, such as Thanksgiving and Easter, were celebrations with family and other guests gathering for meals that provided endless portions of food and treats that became part of our annual traditions to this day. Christmas was a special time in our house and my father's favorite holiday. He would spend weeks after work carefully planning out the decorations that would adorn the house, and he took pride in his Christmas Eve parties known as the "Night of Magic," proudly playing the holiday tunes of Bing Crosby to the background of the Yule Log program on the television. Midnight Mass on Christmas Eve was an occasional event if we managed to stay awake long enough to attend and even more special if I served as an altar boy, which I did once or twice during those years. Christmas morning found us spending hours sifting through what seemed like a mountain of gifts under the tree. My parents were of modest means but didn't hold back on their desire to provide us with everything they could for the holiday. I always felt this was their way of making sure we had the Christmas that they wished they had as children. It was by far our favorite time of the year.

Our lives were blessed with a sort of expected normalcy that comes from working hard, making good decisions, and following the "golden rule." But that was not to make us immune from the randomness of life's cruelty. There were signs that things were about to change.

Timmy had been displaying signs of health anomalies that raised some concerns. As he grew, he remained noticeably thin and unable to put on weight. One of our neighbors affectionately nicknamed him "Bones" because of his appearance. His appetite would be best described as finicky, which we felt could have been his aversion to certain foods, but it never seemed to improve. He started to experience headaches that ranged from mild to severe. My parents took him to doctors to seek answers to the headaches and lack of appetite, only to be told, somewhat dismissively, to serve him milkshakes to supplement his caloric intake. "He needs to put on weight," they would say as if we didn't know. My parents' intuition led them to continue to consult with doctors to see if there was something else to be concerned about.

Parents in general have an intuition about their children when they can sense things are not quite right. My parents were not naïve and possessed that same intuitive sense. They knew this was not normal and were concerned, but to us, they remained generally positive even if they were getting increasingly alarmed. Eventually, one doctor felt Timmy needed further tests as he suspected there could be a more concrete reason for these symptoms. The headaches were real, and his appetite was minimal, so there had to be a cause.

It was June of 1973, right around the day of my eighth grade graduation from St. Francis Grammar School. My parents had taken my brother to be examined by specialists and undergo tests. With my mother and brother remaining at the hospital, my father arrived home to share some very unexpected results. No matter how good your intuition is or how prepared you think you are, some news hits you with such force and in such a profound way that you instantly realize everything you knew about a normal life is about to change in a way you never saw coming.

I was in the kitchen when my father came home. Walking in the side door and into the kitchen, he was visibly shaken but trying to hold it together. Without saying hello, he delivered the devastating news. Fighting back tears he barely made it through the sentence that was about to change our lives. "Your brother has a brain tumor!" Hand over his face and sobbing, he found my sister in the living room and let her know as well. Not only was this not what we wanted to hear, but even more terrifying was that it was the first time I had ever seen my father cry. This was a man who seemed to handle every challenge and adversity in his life with determined strength and optimism. Seeing him like this only amplified my concerns. I was confused, blindsided, and afraid, for I did not know what was going to happen from here.

From the moment I heard this diagnosis, my head was spinning. I felt nauseous, with overwhelming thoughts and emotions, and wondered if this was actually happening. I remember not knowing how to react. Was I supposed to cry, scream, or get angry? My reaction, not unexpected considering my temperament, was anger. I remember blurting out something to the effect of "Oh God" and pounded my fist into the refrigerator door several times with such force that it is no small wonder I didn't break my hand. For some unknown reason, I just ran out through the front door and sat on the curb of the street, staring into nowhere. I'm not sure I completely grasped the severity of this situation, but playing off my father's reaction, I was scared to death. This was more of a fear of the unknown than it was of anything known, which was not much.

Al "Lefty" Gore, our neighbor and my father's best friend, must have heard the news and came over to see my father. He ran past me saying, "It's going to be okay; it's going to okay." It didn't seem okay. I was trying to make sense of it all, but since I had just turned fourteen, I was incapable of sorting out those thoughts or recognizing what feelings I was supposed to have. I was numb and in shock.

My sister came out of the house and started walking down to the church to pray. I sat by the street. She went looking for God. Maybe I was hoping he would come to me. In what seemed like an instant, this moment was to be the beginning of a journey that would challenge our strength as a family and test our faith in medicine, in each other, and, yes, in God.

Chapter 4

AN ARDUOUS JOURNEY BEGINS

One side effect of experiencing a life-changing event is that my memory from this day forward was void of most experiences that were not associated with my brother's illness and subsequent treatments. I do not remember my eighth grade graduation ceremony. No recollection whatsoever. I cannot recall if the news of my brother's illness came before or after the ceremony, but I do know the two events were closely linked in time. There is one picture I have seen showing me in the school-colored green cap and gown proceeding into the church with my classmates, so it provides evidence that I was there. It's as if my memory bank was purged of nonessential information to free up storage as one would do for a computer hard drive. There was this fog that settled into my brain for the next couple of years that prevented me from consolidating many of my experiences from that day through the early years in high school. If prompted by pictures or through reminiscing with friends, some disconnected shreds of information or specific people sneak through, but overall, if it didn't involve my brother's struggles, any information or events over the next two and a half years deemed irrelevant were dismissed.

That summer of 1973, Timmy was sent to the Albert Einstein College of Medicine in the Bronx, New York (now part of the Montefiore Medical system). There he was to begin a plan of treatment that would include the first of three major surgeries he would need to endure to mitigate, remove, or destroy the tumor. His surgeon, Dr. Kenneth Shulman, who we were told was one of the top pediatric neurological surgeons who served at several Bronx hospitals and Department Chair at the Albert Einstein College of Medicine in New York, was assigned to the case.[1] It is notable to remember that this was early 1970s medicine. Certain technologies that we see as ubiquitous in the modern medical toolkit today were years if not a few decades away from being deployed in hospitals. Laser surgery, imaging techniques, and targeted, individually specific chemotherapies were unknown to us and not available as an option. We hoped that Dr. Shulman and his team could get inside and surgically remove the tumor and just send us back to continue our "normal" life. My parents packed up and made plans to stay for the duration of the surgery and recovery.

My sister and I were sent to stay with my aunt Nancy, known to others as Sister Mary Catherine, who was a professor of Spanish at Georgian Court College (now University) in Lakewood, New Jersey. The campus was closed for summer recess with only a handful of nuns and other staff tending to the operations. The historic and bucolic setting was eerily devoid of any activity, giving it a calm, yet somewhat creepy feel. We stayed in one of the dorm buildings, ate in the dining hall, and took advantage of the opportunity to swim in the Casino pool and play basketball in the gym. I would dribble my basketball around campus, stopping to read the plaques that identified the variety of tree species lining this idyllic setting. It could be a bit boring to young teens, but it did provide a quiet and calm setting for us to decompress and find some positive distractions under the circumstances.

As the nation was captivated by the Congressional hearings on Watergate in Washington, D.C., which were being televised, we prayed and waited for the phone call that would give us the results of the surgery happening in the Bronx. The options for treatment were standard for the time. The first step was surgery followed by radiotherapy and, if needed, chemotherapy, which in the 1960s and early 1970s became another tool in the treatment of pediatric cancer. Although chemotherapy has been around in some form since the 1940s, its availability for widespread use was just beginning, which translates, in my mind, to still being experimental. We were going to try it all if needed. We had to.

One late afternoon, we received a phone call with the news that we had been waiting for and keeping us on edge. The ideal result was that the tumor would be removed, and after follow-up treatment Timmy would be good to go. The crisis resolved, right? Unfortunately, that was not to be the case. My aunt took the call from my parents and calmly listened to the results. The tumor was determined to be inoperable as it was located in a sensitive area behind his left eye, wrapped around the optic nerve and precariously close to the pituitary gland. It was described as the size of a walnut and growing. This would explain the increasing severity of the headaches, and the proximity to the pituitary gland may have had something to do with other symptoms related to his growth and appetite. Due to the tumor's location and mass, Dr. Shulman and his team determined that it was too difficult to remove surgically without taking additional and possibly catastrophic risks. Some of the tissue was extracted for biopsy to see if it was malignant or benign. This development would determine the course of his medical treatment going forward. We would hear those results in a day or two, so we did what we had been doing all week—we prayed.

The biopsy result seemed to be the only positive news to favor our situation. The tumor was a type identified as an astrocytoma. We were somewhat relieved when we were told it was benign. It was localized but still growing. It was a small victory that it was not metastasizing where we would have to be concerned about a more aggressive cancer that could spread to other organs and present a much more challenging scenario. So, there was hope, we thought.

In the many years since, my interest in science led me to research this type of tumor and has allowed me to understand what we had been up against. This research also gave me a sense of understanding as to what Timmy had to endure and how even more heroic he was in demonstrating strength and determination in his battle with cancer.

An astrocytoma develops from astrocytes, which are star-shaped cells that make up the supportive tissue of the brain. It is the most common form of primary brain tumor and tends to be low grade (I or II) and slow growing. More specifically, it is known today as pilocytic astrocytoma (or optical pathway glioma), which occurs mostly in children.

According to the American Brain Tumor Association at the University of California San Francisco (UCSF) Brain Tumor Center, pilocytic astrocytomas represent about 15.6 percent of primary brain tumors and 60 percent of all astrocytic tumors in children.[2] In the 1970s, the five-year survival rate from an astrocytoma in adolescents and young adults ranged from 48-71 percent depending on the grade (I, II, III, or IV), type, and other factors. In children (zero to fourteen years of age), the survival rate varied from 71-89 percent in most countries from 1970-2004 (Girardi, Allemani, and Coleman, 2020).[3]

We did not have this information available to us at the time, but had we known, it may have brought some comfort knowing the odds could be in our favor. Today, the ten-year survival rate is approaching 92.2 percent.[4] That is great news for how far medical science has come in treating this disease and should be a source of optimism for the families involved.

Timmy exhibited the requisite symptoms for his type of tumor: headaches, vomiting, nausea, fatigue, weight gain or loss, in his case loss. These signs were prevalent for some time as we were trying to "put a little weight on him" with milkshakes and other high-calorie foods. We never considered that he had developed a tumor; however, my parents were intuitive enough to think this was not just a weight problem. Consequently, the delay in diagnosis may have played a factor in whether any future treatment had a chance to be successful.

Despite the daunting challenge in front of us, we had to prepare for a long and arduous journey for which we had no experience or knowledge to guide us. We were at the mercy of doctors and medical science. But we had our faith, and that was a weapon we felt would carry us through. After all, how could an all-knowing and loving God allow this to happen to one of his children, especially one who envisioned himself as *"...a house of God till the end of the world."*

Although the tumor remained intact, fortunately, so did Timmy's sense of humor and playfulness. When Timmy was in recovery, Dr. Schulman woke him from his anesthesia-induced sleep to assess his condition. He asked him if he would count to ten. Barely conscious Timmy replied, "In what language?" Somewhat confused, Dr. Shulman went out of the room to tell my parents what he said. They replied with a chuckle that it was correct—he could count in three languages. He returned to the room, a little amused that he just got played, and said, "Okay young man, how about English?" Even under the circumstances, Timmy could coax a smile out of anyone.

After the surgery, while Timmy was recovering from this incredibly invasive procedure, we would take several, sometimes harrowing trips on the Cross Bronx Expressway up to the Einstein Medical Center, sometimes staying overnight on weekends, sleeping in a hotel, or passing time in the small waiting rooms lounging on their plastic-covered cushioned furniture (you know the kind that sticks to your skin every time you try to get up) and tolerating the dreadful cafeteria food. When we visited him in the room, it was rather shocking to see his condition compared to when he was last home. He was generally in and out of sleep, unable to communicate. I could not tell if he knew we were there. When the bandages covering the surgical area were changed, I was able to see his shaved head now lined with a grotesque-looking scar that spanned from the top of one ear to the top of the other ear with a circular depression in the left center indicating the place where they removed a portion of his skull to enter his brain. His left bloodshot eye was significantly swollen and displayed a range of discoloration from dark red to blue to purple. IV drips hung from a pole on the side with monitors and tubes completing a disturbing scene that I was not particularly prepared to see. He looked as if he had been in a horrific accident. It was hard to look at and left me weak-kneed and queasy. Although it was upsetting to see him this way, it was also eerily fascinating how a golf-ball-size piece of tissue could do this much damage while remaining so elusive to the surgeons. He was fighting an enemy he could never see.

Throughout the ordeal, my mother stayed with him. She never left his side. She felt every IV setup, every needle, every blood test and radiation treatment, and endured every scream as his headaches would assault him day and night. She was his advocate for medical decisions and would challenge nurses and doctors if she felt her son was being unnecessarily poked and prodded. From day one she was my brother's constant companion whether home or away while my father had to return to work, and we attended school. This had to be a painful and lonely time for her. When she wasn't sleeping or eating, she must have been praying, for the rosary beads lay on the table next to the bed, never far away. That was her nature. This was her son. They were going to battle this together no matter the outcome. She never gave up, not on her faith and certainly, not on her son.

I was starting to develop a level of predictable anxiety whenever I was in a hospital. Since this was my first experience with a medical crisis, it became a standard for my responses in these scenarios. This was to stay with me for many years. It seems that anytime I visited a hospital, for any reason, it was that uncomfortable feeling that would cascade over my body and leave me agitated and nervous, as if bad news was waiting to greet me just around the corner. Young teens are vulnerable emotionally and physically. Having to address my own adolescent issues was hard enough, and the current circumstances were adding to an increasing level of distress.

This whole experience was overwhelming. I did not have the life experience to fall back on or the maturity to navigate the changes. I couldn't share my feelings with my parents; the Lord only knows what they were going through. I had to be strong and show that I could handle it. After all, I was the oldest son. My little brother was suffering, my parents were in crisis, and I had to grow up. I stayed silent and tried to deal with it as best I could. But I wasn't dealing with it. I just wanted it to be over so we could return to the other life that we had. Little did I know those days were long gone.

Chapter 5

A CROWN OF THORNS

Toward the end of that summer, Timmy was released from the hospital to come home and recover, and I thought, *Recover from what?* The tumor was still in his head! But it was still better than being in a hospital, getting jabbed every hour and dosed with whatever levels of radiation the medical staff prescribed. Maybe all that medication and radiation was going to have some benefit that would free him from this hell he was experiencing. I couldn't help but wonder what a now ten-year-old boy was thinking about all of this. One day you're home playing records, watching comedy shows, going to school, and the next day you're having holes drilled into your skull, your brain pushed around, followed by a five-course meal of pain medications and steroids. It seemed to happen so fast.

The day he arrived home, my sister and I, along with our incredible neighbors, set up a modest welcome home celebration. We had signs hung from the window and the door, and we played music—one of his favorite songs, "Joy to the World" by the band Three Dog Night. Timmy slowly emerged from the car. He was thin with an ashen complexion, wearing a hat to cover that awful scar. We clapped and cheered as he started to carefully walk up the front steps so as not to stumble. He was weak and unsure of himself, which was to be expected. Hearing the music, his eyes welled up with tears as he tried to smile. I'm sure all of us had tears. It had been a long summer.

Our house was rather small. It had two bedrooms, one bathroom, and a five-by-nine-foot glorified closet—just big enough to put a bed into—that my sister used as her room. It was not fair, but she made it work. Timmy and I shared a bedroom. It was a place where two brothers could talk, laugh, argue, play records, attack each other with projectiles and pillows, and even compete to see who could make the loudest farting noises before getting the "knock it off and go to sleep" warning coming through the wall from my parents' room. We would talk about anything and everything, especially at night when we couldn't sleep.

Being a big brother was a role I cherished. It made me feel important that I had a little responsibility in setting a good example for him as he grew up. I looked forward to teaching him to play sports (which he was not really that interested in anyway), drive a car, change a tire, ask a girl out on a date, buy him his first drink, and whatever else was required by an older sibling. I felt very comfortable in this role. We all had our roles. My sister was the leader and the adult when my parents were not around. I was the irritant, ball-playing prankster who generally tried, maybe not hard enough, to stay out of trouble, and Timmy was the chosen one. That was it. And it was just fine with us.

Timmy's Wish still hung on the dining room wall. It seemed to take on a different meaning after his diagnosis. I stopped one day to read it yet again, trying to glean some message from it. What did it mean? What was he trying to say? I had a gnawing feeling there was some connection here between his wish and his illness. I was old enough to ask the questions but too young to figure out the answers.

During some of our late nights when Timmy was not able to sleep, which was quite often, we would talk a little about how he was feeling. His headaches were still there. He felt the pressure building at times and said his head felt heavy. He never downplayed his condition. He seemed to know how serious it was, but he kept things in perspective. He had a remarkable capacity to see the big picture for someone his age. There were some thoughts he didn't share, but sometimes he would surprise me. There was one instance when, not surprisingly, I asked a typically dumb question:

"Does it hurt?"

He would answer in a tone of impatient sarcasm,

"I have a brain tumor. What do you think?"

Okay, not the most probing level of inquiry. Maybe it was better to just avoid the subject altogether. I was wading too far into the deep end. Then he would hit me with a sledgehammer.

"Do you think I'm gonna die?" he said so casually and without emotion.

Well, that came out of nowhere. It was so nonchalant that it made it much more disturbing. Fumbling for something to say that would force a redirect, the only thing my less-than-nimble mind could come up with was:

"No, you're not! It's going to be fine. You're going to be fine. Now go to sleep."

"How do you know?" he followed up without hesitation.

Looking for an escape hatch, I suddenly pulled the old "I need to use the bathroom" excuse to buy time so I could come up with some big brother-quality answer that would put this discussion to bed so to speak. I returned from the bathroom only to find him fast asleep. Whew! I had a reprieve, at least for now.

Once again, he showed his depth of contemplation and understanding. I was not thinking that at all. I was blissfully naive to the seriousness of the condition and its underlying complexities. Make no mistake, I knew it was bad, but I always felt he was going to get better. He had to. Why did he bring that up? Dying? Not happening. I was always told God would answer your prayers, right?

When Timmy was finally able to return to school, my parents were concerned that the unsightly scar on the top of his head could upset the other children. They decided to buy him a hairpiece to cover it. I'm not sure why a hat wouldn't do. Maybe it was a school rule, but I was not part of that discussion. It was odd to see him wearing what amounted to a toupee, but at least it covered that hideous scar, which was not easy to look at. Not long thereafter I found out there were a couple of kids in school who were mocking him and his head covering. They were playing with it and pulling at it. This must have been humiliating for him. When I heard about it, I was enraged! My first instinct was to find them and pound out an apology. They needed to pay. This was my little brother, and he had gone through hell, and I was not going to allow him to be picked on for something he had no control over! Timmy implored me not to go find them. His response to me was:

"It really doesn't bother me. I have to deal with chemotherapy. I can deal with this. They're just being stupid."

He was already teaching me the lessons of grace and dignity amid adversity. I felt helpless, but I knew exacting some level of vengeance was not going to make him better. Somehow, he was the one who became the arbiter of reason. I had no way to help him and no way to protect him. He was preparing himself for challenges that were far more grueling than what a few local clowns could dish out.

Timmy's faith was never far from his thoughts, and he would express them in unusual moments. On one of those occasions when his headaches were particularly painful, my father went into his bedroom to check on him and found him crying. He was asked how bad his headache was, and he replied that he now understands how Jesus must have felt when the crown of thorns was placed on his head. Again, in a moment when no one would blame him if he engaged in a little self-indulgent pity, he demonstrated his empathy for another type of suffering, in another time and place. A story of suffering he knew all too well, for he knew all the stories of the Bible and in them must have found a connection and a comfort. His empathy and compassion were becoming his calling card.

Radiation treatment did not seem to slow the growth of the tumor. He was feeling the pressure in his head. There was a buildup of fluid originating from the area surrounding the tumor, causing additional headaches. He was receiving several rounds of low-level chemotherapy applied to his treatment schedule. To relieve the pressure, he would have additional surgeries that would involve implanting a shunt in his brain around the site of the tumor. This would be connected to a subcutaneous tube that would travel over his ear, around his neck, and down into his stomach. It was supposed to drain any excess fluid causing the pressure he felt. Whenever he could feel the pressure building, one of us would use our thumb to pump the button under the skin on top of his head for a count of ten. This became so routine for us that it was not unusual to be sitting at the dinner table with a burger in one hand while pumping his shunt with the other. This was life now. We all had to help and find a way to cope with the medical requirements while pretending it was just another day.

We continued to fight the good fight. My father needed to be at work, and my mother tended to my brother at home in between trips to the hospital for treatment and follow-up exams.

My sister and I went to school during the week and then spent some part of some weekends at a hospital. The neighbors were always there to help and feed us as needed, but we were generally on our own, with Coleen taking responsibility at home. I am not sure how much help I was. I was just trying not to be a problem.

After surgery a return to school

Chapter 6

A BOY ON A MISSION

I finished my freshman year of high school with grades that were mediocre at best. I struggled to maintain focus and any sense of enthusiasm for what I was learning. As stated earlier my recollections of my first three years of high school are virtually nonexistent. I do not have clear memories of classes, events, football games, dances, or anything else related to a typical high school experience. I'm sure I did participate at times, but I cannot summon up those memories. I did know that I was underperforming academically compared to my track record. Socially, academically, and probably emotionally, I was treading water. I don't remember hanging out with friends.

I do remember being cut from the high school basketball team, which was a punch in the gut for someone who loved to play sports and had done so for as long as I can remember. As a result, I lost interest in playing sports and did not try out for any other team at the high school so I could avoid the humiliation of getting cut again. I did, however, join a local basketball team at our CYO that was somewhat competitive and did not involve a great deal of time. Sports was my only refuge, and playing was a constructive diversion. As with my school experiences, my recollection of CYO ball is vague at best. There was too much going on for it to matter anyway.

At home, Timmy continued to battle his illness. He had his good days and bad days. There were nights I would be awakened by the sound of him moaning in his sleep. I couldn't help but wonder if these were dreams or nightmares. What was going on in his brain? On other nights he would startle everyone with a scream as his headaches would sometimes go from dull to piercing. One night he begged me to "make it stop, please make it stop!" All I or my parents could do was pump the shunt to alleviate the pressure and hold him until he was exhausted enough to go back to sleep. We were somewhat helpless to alleviate his suffering.

I felt so bad for him, my parents, and my sister. This version of the American Dream was becoming a nightmare. I buried my head under the pillow as if trying to hide from the reality of it all and started praying. "Hail Mary, full of Grace, the Lord is with thee..." over and over. If I just kept praying, maybe there would be some kind of divine intervention. Maybe, but since it hadn't happened already, I was not holding my breath.

Not all of Timmy's days were taxing. When he was feeling well enough, he would get outside and play like everyone else. A little taller but still very thin and fragile looking, he would occasionally join me and my friends in a game of Wiffle ball or touch football that we would play in someone's yard or in the street. We would devise plays that would hand him the ball and dramatically trip over ourselves pretending we were trying to tackle him while he scampered to the telephone pole marking the boundary for a touchdown. We would all clap and congratulate him on his impressive feat as he sheepishly looked at us knowing full well that we were faking it. He enjoyed it anyway.

There were also times when he demonstrated that he was thinking on a different level from anyone else. One day, during a game of street Wiffle ball, we assigned him to be the first baseman. This allowed him to play without exerting too much effort and kept him away from the occasional car that would pass through. In the middle of the game, we suddenly noticed we had no first baseman! He just disappeared, gone, nowhere to be found. We called out a few times to no avail. Despite our annoyance, we kept playing. Maybe he just got tired and went home. After an hour or so, it was time for dinner, and Timmy walked in the door as if everything was just fine. I was chastising him for leaving us without a player and interrogating him as to his whereabouts. My mother demanded an answer because, of course, under the circumstances, we needed to know where he was at all times. He let us know he went to visit Mrs. Errickson, the elderly woman who lived across the street. For what purpose? he was asked. He said he thought she was lonely and needed someone to talk to.

This was not typical behavior for an eleven-year-old boy. And it was not the only time. Another friendly but quiet elderly neighbor on our street, Harold Painter, would be seen sitting on his porch sporting his trademark black-rimmed, Coke-bottle lens glasses watching us play ball and applauding the occasional great play from the asphalt field. From time to time, you would see Timmy sitting next to him on the porch, engaged in quiet conversation for what seemed to be hours. They seemed to enjoy each other's company, although it was a mystery as to what they would talk about. Mr. Painter would tell my father how much he enjoyed their talks. This was another indication that Timmy had a bond, a special connection to adults, especially those who could appreciate his gift. It was as if he was on a mission to share his kindness with those who needed it the most. He was building a reputation and, apparently, a following.

We were fortunate to have access to a newly constructed municipal pool complex at the far end of town, complete with Olympic size swimming areas and other amenities, that gave us a place to cool off and hang out with friends during the hot summer months. My mother would take Timmy there from time to time depending on how he felt so he could interact and feel like a normal kid for a few hours. On one of those occasions, Timmy met a woman named Elisabeth who happened to take an interest in him. After a couple of these encounters, Elisabeth felt she should introduce herself to my mother. They began a conversation and then a friendship. Elisabeth told her that Timmy reminded her of her son. It was revealed that she lost her son to a type of kidney disorder. They began to share stories of their experiences and developed a bond that only mothers in these situations could understand. Elisabeth became a source of comfort and emotional refuge for my mother. She had been where my mother was going, and her support was going to be needed.

Timmy had an extraordinary ability to bring people together. This random meeting between two souls who developed a friendship based on their common struggle, maybe wasn't so random. It eventually crossed my mind that maybe Timmy was looking out for the one person who shared every minute of every day with him on his journey and at the same time giving Elisabeth an opportunity to turn her grief into a purpose. They needed each other and Timmy seemed to understand that.

38 ★ *Timmy's Wish*

The three of us in 1974

There were other incidents we did not witness but found out about that continued to reveal the character of this unusual child. One day at school he decided to cut recess and go to church instead. The school was connected to the church via an enclosed walkway, and the students ate lunch in the cafeteria located below the church. So, taking the easy detour, Timmy went to his favorite place.

After entering the church through the side door, he turned to where parishioners could light a candle, make an offering, and say a quiet prayer. He happens to meet a woman doing the same and told her his name and said he was sick and wished to light a candle, but he had no money for the offering. In many Catholic churches, there are containers nearby for donations you could make for each candle lit. The woman gave him some money; he lit a candle and then thanked her, adding that she reminded him of his mother. The woman, who was impressed with this child, eventually shared this unusual encounter with my mother; otherwise, we may not have known this had happened.

I wonder how many other encounters there may have been that remain unknown to us. Timmy seemed to understand the pain, loss, loneliness, or sadness others were experiencing. He had a special sense and a gift that made him unique. He was touching lives but was he—maybe—even building his church and amassing his congregation to fulfill his Wish?

In that summer of 1974, my parents decided to take us all on a trip to Disney World in Florida, which had opened up just a few years before, to give Timmy a break from his treatments and provide all of us with a much-needed vacation. This was a time to just have some fun and share a positive experience at one of the most desirable destinations for families. Tim loved Disney and all the movies, cartoons, characters, and songs. This was to be the trip of a lifetime, and, remarkably, my parents found a way to make it happen despite their financial challenges at the time. I wonder if they felt this could be the last opportunity for all of us to have a vacation together considering my brother's declining condition. If it was, you couldn't come up with a better place to go.

To save money we traveled down by train. But the nearly twenty-hour trip, with the jostling and the vibrations of the ride and the struggle to get adequate sleep, took its toll on Tim. He had difficulty walking and maintaining his balance and stamina, so arrangements were made to acquire a wheelchair, and we scheduled our time in the park around his ability to handle activities and shows. He smiled the whole time, beaming at meeting the characters and watching the parades. He had to be uncomfortable, though he didn't seem to show it. Sitting in his wheelchair, he watched the daily parades while the characters would come up and shake his hand or give him a hug. He must have felt like a celebrity himself. He enjoyed whatever rides he could tolerate and had the time of his life. During our stay, he didn't have to think about hospitals, surgeries, bloodwork, or treatments.

It was a great vacation for all of us, and we needed it. To avoid the train, we rented a car for an even longer ride home, which was another adventure in and of itself, but the memories of the whole experience were a net positive for all of us. It felt like we were a normal family again, at least for a few days.

One event foretold for me that things may not be getting better but, in fact, much worse. That same summer, Timmy would sometimes take the short walk down the park at the local elementary school to participate in the seasonal recreation program held by the town. A little bit of independence was good for him and gave him a few hours where he could just be a normal kid. He played kickball and knock-hockey (a popular tabletop game) or made crafts under the tent until he was tired, and then made his way home.

There was one day that I walked down to the park to get him to come home for lunch. On our walk back he developed a panicked look on his face. I asked him what was wrong. He said in a worried voice: "I have to go!"

"What do you mean you have to go?" I said.

Showing a growing desperation, he blurted out, "I have to go, I have to go! Get me home! Get me home!" This time, I understood what he meant.

"Why don't you just go in the bushes? I'll watch—nobody will see you," I replied, trying to calm him down.

By this time, he was getting pretty upset with me and with his eyes welling up yelled, "I'm not going in the bushes! I have to go number two! *Just—get—me—home!*"

So, we started walking, but he was clearly becoming extremely uncomfortable and moved slowly. I wanted to pick up the pace, so I began to carry him, piggyback style, and quickly resumed the short walk home. He was surprisingly light. I could feel his bony arms and legs wrapped around me as I increased the pace to a slow jog. It became more urgent when I sensed, and smelled, that he was losing control of his bowels. He started to cry and pleaded with me to go faster. I was going as fast as I could but not fast enough.

We finally arrived home. I called for my mother, who helped him up the stairs to the bathroom. She helped him out of his soiled clothes and put him in the shower. The smell was as intense as it was nauseating. It seemed as if the medications and everything else inside of him were pouring out of his body without warning. My mother looked concerned but for some reason not as panicked as I was. Maybe she was becoming numb to dealing with yet another in a long line of side effects of his treatments. He was embarrassed and I was embarrassed for him. He was losing control. He had, up until this time, handled his illness like a trooper. This was the first time I saw real fear in his eyes. "Please don't tell anyone!" he begged. "Please!" This had never happened before, and I had the growing feeling that things were going to get much worse.

Chapter 7

HAIL MARY

As 1974 turned into 1975, Timmy's struggles continued. He was to be sent to Mercy Fitzgerald Medical Center, a teaching hospital in Upper Darby, Pennsylvania, a western suburb of Philadelphia, for what we eventually learned was to be a final attempt to arrest or destroy the tumor that had tortured my brother for the last eighteen months. He was assigned to Dr. Isaac Djerassi, a medical researcher and clinician who played a role in the development of centrifuge filtration techniques and white cell transfusion to support aggressive cancer chemotherapy. He also pioneered research in high methotrexate chemotherapy.[1] Certainly, he was an accomplished expert in the field, which at this point is the kind of person you would want on your case. It was also a sign that this may be a last-chance scenario—a Hail Mary pass if you will. He was the one who you go to when you have no other place to go.

Although we were not privy to the actual discussion, my father hinted to us that Timmy may be getting the largest dose of chemotherapy ever administered to a child of his age. Whether this was accurate or not, it was undoubtedly an experimental dose. This seemed drastic, but I surmised that the idea was to kill the tumor with the chemotherapy and hope it didn't kill him first. At least that is how I understood it.

What a dilemma for my parents! Having to be told that doctors were going to aggressively attack the growing tumor, knowing that there was the possibility that it would not work, and what that result would mean was a scenario that would buckle the knees of any parent and present an unthinkable moral and ethical dilemma. Do you decline the treatment and sit by while this tumor continues to grow and your son's condition slowly and painfully declines, helpless to do anything to stop it? Or do you take the chance, however small, that this could work and deal with short- and long-term side effects of the treatment, not knowing what this would put a child through and what his quality of life would be if he survived? Timmy had suffered so much. How much more was he going to have to endure? As a parent, I could never come close to imagining their utter anguish when faced with that scenario and what strength they found to give their consent to the doctor's strategy. They must have felt there was no choice.

My parents trusted Dr. Djerassi. They had to. He was the expert and their only hope at this time. Soft-spoken and empathic, he prepared them for what was to come. They were told very clearly the reality of either moving ahead or doing nothing at all. I often thought how difficult it was for him to determine the course of action in case after case, patient after patient, family after family, delivering good news and bad news. He had his own purpose, I'm sure—to move medical research forward and that it would hopefully lead to the alleviation of the suffering that surrounded him daily. It was a challenging time for all involved.

Ultimately, my parents agreed to go forward with the treatment, put their faith in God and in medicine, and pray for a miracle.

Mercy Hospital, I remember at the time, was a welcoming and caring environment. During our time there Timmy and my parents established friendly relationships with the hardworking medical staff. The nurses on all shifts were attentive, and we knew them on a first-name basis. As with everyone who came to know Timmy, they became very fond of him. He had a way of making people smile, and his strength throughout his ordeal was an inspiration to any who came to know him. The personal care demonstrated by the nurses toward him and my parents during this time was greatly appreciated. They understood the difficulties we were going through. They made us feel special, even though they were surrounded in this hospital by many other families in similar circumstances.

If it hadn't already, the severity of the situation became very clear to me when one day on a visit, I decided to take a break and go for a walk around the hospital floor. Leaving my brother's room, I took the long way around to extend my time and began to see what the reality of our situation was becoming. There were children slowly walking the hall, holding hands with a parent on one side and gripping a rolling IV stand on the other hand to stabilize their gait. Others were being pushed in wheelchairs. One boy, draped in a loosely fitted hospital gown, shuffled his way along, staring blankly ahead with empty eyes and a pale, expressionless face disturbingly swollen from steroid medications. Next to him was his mother, looking tired and sad, embracing his arm as he cautiously made his way down the hall. Others were sleeping in their darkened rooms with their tiny bodies tethered to monitors and entangled in a web of tubing that provided oxygen and medication. It was a grotesquely quiet and somber atmosphere with the silence only penetrated by sounds of beeping and whooshing cascading through the hall from a vast array of medical equipment clogging each room.

I am not sure how, but I came to learn that these children had a variety of illnesses such as leukemia, liver cancer, and other horrific afflictions of pediatric cancer, and they were here undergoing treatment.

Mercy Hospital was a teaching hospital, meaning it was also a research facility that could accept patients in difficult health circumstances when the typical radiotherapy and surgeries of the day were unsuccessful. The 1970s saw the advent of chemotherapy treatment for pediatric cancers. Mercy Hospital was one of those facilities where experimental medicines and techniques would be employed that would one day become the norm in pediatric care. After a few moments, and after seeing the children and their parents struggling with their afflictions, holding out whatever hope any new treatment could provide and release them from this hell they found themselves in, I suddenly realized where I was. This was the cancer ward for children running out of options. None of them looked well. In fact, they looked worse than that. *This must be where you go when you have no other place to go.*

I was beginning to understand that many of these children were probably not going home. A sick, nauseating feeling came over me that I will never forget. In one short moment and for the first time, it was clear that Timmy may not be coming home either. So now what? Was this really a final longshot attempt to arrest his tumor? And what were the odds? What if he didn't come home? What if none of these children went home? What was this all about then? My fifteen-year-old brain was overwhelmed with the possibility that all along he never had a chance. Everything was running through my mind: hopes and prayers, hopes and prayers! Maybe I didn't pray hard enough or often enough. What did he do to deserve this? He had a Wish, he was different, and he was going to have an impactful life. Why him?

Returning to the room, I looked at Timmy with a different perspective, a different and darker outlook. But maybe and hopefully I was wrong. I wanted to ask so many questions, but, as usual, I kept my thoughts and my concerns to myself. I didn't want to cause any trouble. Had to be strong, you know. Had to handle this. Just keep praying, stay out of trouble, be supportive. *It's going to be okay; it's going be okay*. That's what I kept telling myself.

Chapter 8

"I WISH I WERE A CHURCH..."

My parents remained hopeful that the decision they made would finally bring a path to recovery into focus. They continued to provide as much normalcy for my sister and me as the situation allowed. We continued to go to school and would visit on the occasional weekend. My mother stayed with Timmy every hour, every day, and would do so for as long as it was necessary. Her strength, sacrifice, and faith were inspirational, and she would need every ounce of all of it moving forward.

The treatments commenced, and soon it was understood that Timmy's body was not going to handle the aggressive chemotherapy. Several rounds over several weeks were administered intravenously to a frail and failing body. It was hard not to wonder if this was really worth it. But how could anyone not take whatever chance was offered, even if it was a hope and a prayer? Not going ahead with treatment was giving up, and that was not an option.

March 31, 1975, was Easter Sunday, and the entire family spent the day at the hospital celebrating the Resurrection of

48 ★ *Timmy's Wish*

Jesus and trying to make a difficult situation more hopeful with prayers, photos, and visitors. Timmy was bedridden and tired. He didn't smile much if at all. He tried to accommodate the attempt of a photo op by forcing a labored smile through his cheeks swollen from his various medications.

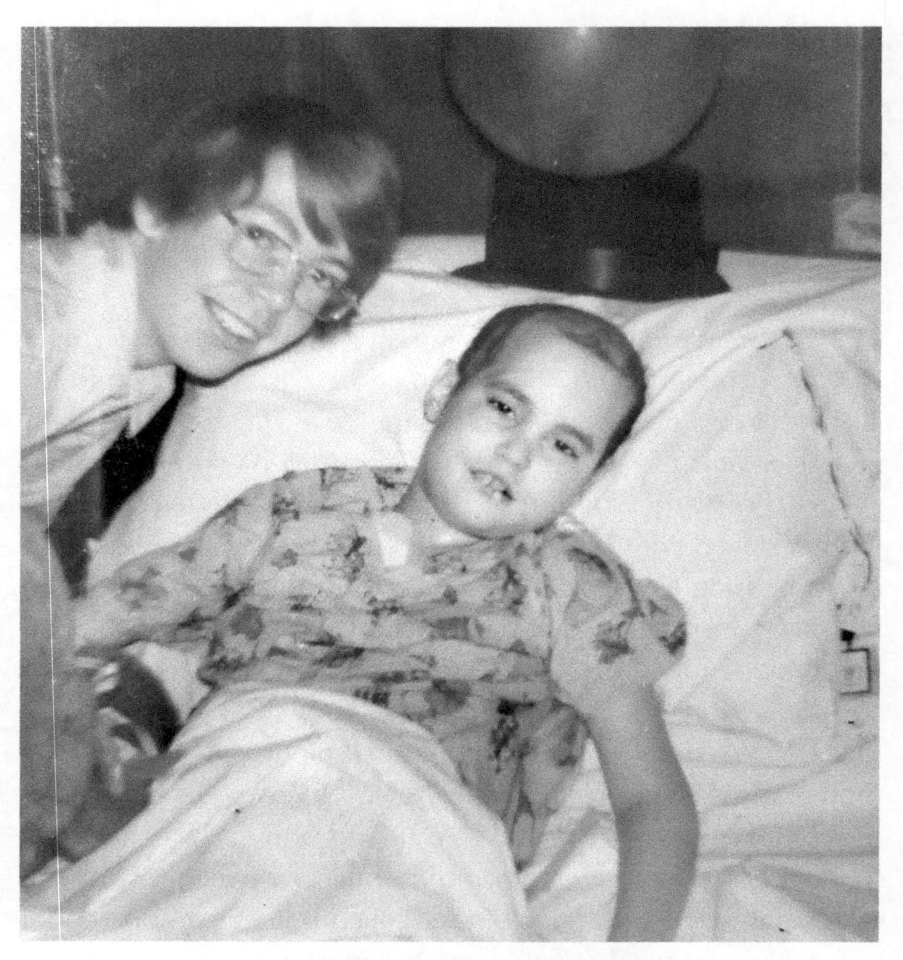

Two brothers Easter Sunday 1975

The following week, April 9th, Timmy celebrated his twelfth birthday, complete with balloons, birthday hats, and a cake.

There were many visitors, including many of the nurses who cared for him over the months, each getting their picture taken with him. He tried to stay awake, but he was so weak and slept through much of the festivities. The reality was never far from everyone's thoughts, but the nursing staff made the whole event so much easier to bear. Their laughter and smiles and willingness to be with us at this moment were a credit to their compassion and how they felt about Timmy. I never thought about if this could be his last birthday. I refused to look at it in that way.

Another celebration took place shortly thereafter. The hospital was visited by His Eminence John Joseph Cardinal Krol, Archbishop of Philadelphia, one of the highest-ranking clerical figures in the country and advisor to the Pope. He was there to administer the Sacrament of Confirmation to another boy at the hospital. My parents were made aware of his visit and asked if the cardinal could do the same for their son. Timmy was scheduled to make his Confirmation that year but was not going to be able to attend the ceremony due to his illness, so this was a wonderful opportunity. Their request was granted. Timmy was not conscious and had not been so for some time but, for whatever reason, at this moment, managed to open his eyes and speak with the archbishop who prayed with him and performed the required ritual for the occasion. Timmy told him what Confirmation name he had selected (it was, not surprisingly, a biblical name—David), repeated the required prayers, and received the Sacrament. This was a special moment for a young boy who cherished his religion and was able to participate in a final expression of his faith.

We traveled back and forth from home to the hospital as often as needed. There were a couple of emergency trips under a "this could be it" scenario. It was not easy on anyone. Close calls, news of tough nights, and no real improvement in his condition, in fact just the opposite. The weight of this had to be unbearable for the rest of my family. For me, I almost expected the worst because nothing was working. Not chemo, not the hopes and prayers, nothing. Just wait and wait some more. "It's going to be okay, right?"

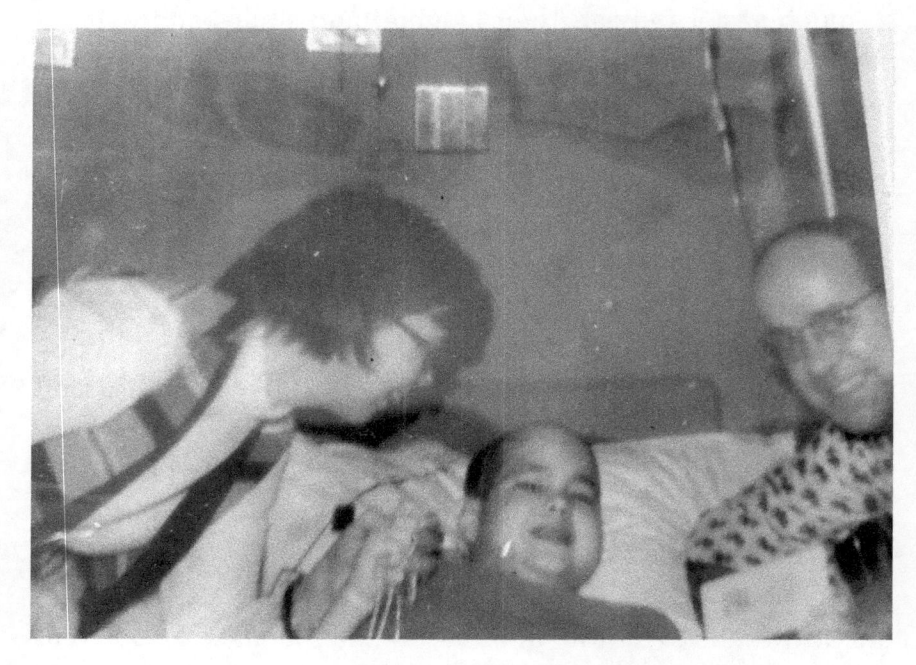

Mom, Dad, and Timmy on his Confirmation Day.

Friday evening, on April 18th, my parents were at the hospital, and our neighbor, the reliable Al Gore, came into the house and told my sister and me that he was going down to the hospital. Another routine trip? Possibly. There was always this feeling that each trip could be a final trip. Oddly, this one felt a bit different. We arrived at the hospital and were taken to Timmy's room. He was unconscious, on his back, looking like he was sleeping, but didn't appear to be in much pain. The atmosphere, however, was noticeably somber. They must know something.

The nurses were not far away, popping in and out to check his vitals. What was unusual was that there was a growing number of visitors showing up. To our knowledge my parents were not directly in contact with everyone, but curiously, my aunt Nancy from Georgian Court College, my uncle John, and his wife, Fanny, who were very fond of Timmy, traveled down from Long Island on a whim, and our close neighbors, Al and Ann Gore, along with me and my sister Coleen, all those he loved and cared about were present at this crucial moment. Was this a coincidence? Were they summoned somehow, or did they have a sense of what was to come?

We were all standing there making small talk, listening to conversations about what the doctors had said, and none of it seemed comforting. It was a dreadful, agonizing experience. I was thinking that at some point we would go home again and wait for the next "this could be it" moment.

We didn't have to wait long. Around eight o'clock that Friday evening, you could see Timmy's face slowly begin to turn red around the cheeks. I heard someone say that maybe he had been or was now running a fever. A nurse came in and took his temperature; then with an abrupt and startling tone of urgency, she blurted out, "He has a temperature; it's 105 degrees!" The light chatter was replaced by a stunned silence and a few gasps as the nurse quickly threw off his blanket and called for help.

In an instant, several staff members rushed in, and one nurse with a stethoscope determined his heart had stopped and he was not breathing. They began pumping air into his mouth through an emergency Ambu bag and asked that everyone leave the room. My parents stood off to the side, holding each other desperately, seeming to know what was happening. I stood near the end of the bed, frozen, just watching the frenzy of activity surrounding my brother, completely overwhelmed by what had just taken place. I was terrified yet kept watching in what I can only describe as a sort of morbid sense of awe.

Before I could leave the room, suddenly, as in a flip of a switch, this flurry of activity stopped. Just like that. They took away the Ambu bag and began to usher those of us who remained behind out of the room. I looked over at my parents holding each other and sobbing. I could hear my father through his tears telling my mother "Let him go, let him go. He's not suffering anymore." This was only the second time I saw my father cry. My brother's face just a moment earlier flushed red with fever was now slowly fading into a pale bluish gray as life drained from his body. He looked relaxed, calm, and at peace.

That's it? It's over? What the hell just happened?

I didn't know what to do. I remember someone, maybe a nurse, taking my arm and guiding me next door. Amidst the sobbing heard around me, the nurse asked if I wanted a cup of water. I don't remember crying. I don't remember talking. I was probably in shock after what I had just witnessed. Taking the small paper cup of water in my hand, I became aware of how this was affecting me. I brought the cup to my mouth, but I was unable to drink as my hand was shaking uncontrollably and I was spilling water on the floor. How was I supposed to act? I had never seen anyone die before. Why wasn't I crying? I just started watching everyone around me to see how they were reacting. This was so surreal, so unexpected, so confusing. What happened to all of those hopes and prayers? Why didn't they work?

From the hall, I could see my parents, still in the room, only this time sitting in conversation with Dr. Djerassi, who had just walked in. I could tell he was consoling them, and through their tears, they were discussing another difficult decision they had to make.

I found out later that Dr. Djerassi asked my parents if they would agree to allow him and his staff to do an autopsy of Timmy's brain for research they were doing into these types of tumors and the effects of the treatments administered. They agreed and had to sign yet another set of papers. Sitting next to their son who had just passed after twenty-two months of pain and suffering, they had to gather whatever strength they had left to engage in this discussion and make a heart-wrenching, unselfish choice to support medical research. I guess something good had to come from this nightmare.

We were allowed to go back into the room and say our final goodbyes. Through his tears, my father kept looking at Timmy, commenting on how peaceful he looked. I couldn't disagree. For the first time in a very long time, he was pain-free. His mouth showed what I thought to be a very subtle smile. I wonder if he really did get his Wish.

The ninety-minute ride home seemed like hours. The dark and eerily empty New Jersey Turnpike was a perfect metaphor for our mood. Inside the car, it was silent as the four of us had to process what had just taken place. My parents were physically and emotionally exhausted. I have no idea how my father was able to pull himself together in order to drive home that night. Losing a loved one is hard enough, but losing a child is a special kind of pain—a distinctly different version of hell. All I remember thinking was how unfair all of this was. Nobody deserved this, not Timmy, not my parents, not my sister, nobody. But we were not the only ones. The hospital had a whole wing of children and their families who were going through this ordeal. Were they next?

I had a lot of questions and I wanted answers. I questioned medicine. I questioned everything we were told about medicine. I questioned hope and prayers, I questioned my religion, and yes, I even questioned God! And oh, I can hear them now as the faithful offer their condolences, "Heaven needed another angel." Bullshit! Heaven has plenty of angels. We need them here. Has anybody looked around lately? Or "God takes those whose job is done." Bullshit again! Timmy was just getting started. He didn't even get a chance! And my favorite response when one doesn't know what to say, "God works in mysterious ways." What a cop-out! None of this would be consoling, but this is what they are going to say, and I wasn't buying any of it.

All these thoughts and more were going through my head, gnawing at me, on that quiet ride home. I was so confused and angry, felt betrayed and worried about how this would affect our family going forward. I had never been through this before, and I had to find a way to deal with it because the next few days were going to be rough.

Chapter 9

"...AND I WOULD JOIN THEM IN PRAYER."

Over the next few days, the wake and the funeral became a testament to Timmy's legacy. My parents anticipated a large crowd and found a funeral home that could accommodate a multiple-day viewing. They were wise to do so. For two days, for four long hours each, there seemed to be a never-ending stream of visitors. Family, friends, neighbors, community members from the school, church, and other related organizations along with classmates, coworkers, and nurses from Mercy Hospital and many who we had never even met came to pay their respects to this twelve-year-old boy and his family. Some of them came on both days to lend their support.

My parents stood there stoically, each day, each hour, and made sure they greeted, thanked, hugged, and cried with each of them. I was in awe of their resilience considering the enormous grief they were feeling. I wanted none of this, however, and kept making excuses to take a walk. More questions came to mind: *Why do we have to go through this? Why do my parents have to go through this?* I found this wake to be a morose and agonizing ritual. Standing next to an open casket for hours, greeting people who were trying hard to say the right words—commenting on how good my brother looked, as if being dead came with a scale of beauty to measure—was a dreadful experience. This ordeal, as with my time in hospitals, made going to any wake an unsettling event for many years. It was just adding to the list of experiences that were to impact my ability to cope.

The funeral itself was a celebration that one would expect for a high-profile individual or dignitary rather than a twelve-year-old. St. Francis Church, Timmy's church, was filled with parishioners from all over the community along with friends and family who had traveled a distance to be there. The echoes of Timmy's Wish hung in the air: *I wish I were a church and if I were, I would sit on the ground watching people coming into me. And I would join them in prayer...*

Several priests officiated the Mass, and one of the nuns from the school beautifully and poignantly sang some of Timmy's favorite hymns, which included "The Prayer of St. Francis" and "Let There Be Peace on Earth." This was my brother and yet I felt I didn't really know him or at least this version of him. It's like he had a separate life that I was only beginning to understand. He seemed bigger and more important that day. How could a twelve-year-old boy from an ordinary family have this impact on so many people?

It was a beautiful service. I was unaware of just how many people attended until Communion was served and we witnessed the seemingly endless procession of congregants, hands folded in reverence, slowly walk past to receive the sacrament. They just kept coming! Timmy would have loved this. Nothing like a Celebration Mass with hundreds of your closest friends and admirers. After Mass, we led a long convoy of cars on a short ride to Resurrection Cemetery in Piscataway for the burial and our final goodbyes. We greeted our guests and well-wishers at the repast luncheon and returned home. It was over. All of it. I couldn't help but think, now what?

My experience at Mercy Hospital left a significant impact on me. My exposure to illness and mortality, the suffering of others, the heroic efforts of medical staff, the shared faith and love of family and friends facing adversity, the medical discussions, and the dignified and compassionate manner in which doctors and nurses dealt with death was humbling. It was an education I did not ask for but maybe one that was necessary.

I needed to grow up. I had to face reality and try to deal with it, somehow. Some questions needed answers. Timmy was gone. But what about the rest of us? Just back to work and school, and everything was going to be okay? Well, it wasn't okay. I wasn't okay. I felt different. I was emotionally drained and filled that void with one part confusion mixed with two parts anger. I wanted to do something but didn't know what or how. I'm sure the others in my family were going through their own reality checks, so I didn't want to bother them with my issues. After all, I was trying to be strong for them. At this time in my life, I didn't know what grief or trauma was or how to deal with them. So, like I did with everything else, I kept it inside, put on a happy face, and soldiered on.

My return to an engaged experience in high school didn't happen until my senior year. My brother passed in the spring of my sophomore year, and junior year was a complete blank. I know I was there, but it's like that year was deleted from my mind. Senior year was something different. The fog that clouded my experiences lifted, and I came out of my shell, so to speak, to reengage in the normal events of school life and activities. I started playing sports again, took part in senior prom, the class trip, school clubs, and committees. I interacted socially a bit more, although I was still cautious about whom I associated with, and my interest in science, more apparent now due to my recent experiences, came alive in my biology class.

This was a revelation for me. Getting my hands dirty in the lab, preparing microscope slides to explore the microworld, and doing dissections to examine the macro world, I realized that this may be a path for me to consider. I felt I needed to do something significant. Maybe down the road, I could find a cure for what afflicted my brother. Maybe I could alleviate the pain and suffering of those families we left behind and at the same time exact my revenge on this cancer and bring closure to me and my family. I had to have a purpose. Maybe this was it.

My sister may have had a similar sense of duty. She left for College Misericordia in Pennsylvania that year to study nursing. I'm sure the whole experience of the past couple of years and her observations of the hospital environment must have influenced her decision. I followed the year after and planned to major in Medical Technology at the University of Scranton in Pennsylvania, a highly respected Jesuit institution. My mother was pleased that I was attending a Catholic university and even teasingly quipped, "Those Jesuits will straighten you out." It was her way of saying she knew I would be fine there.

Nestled within the hills of Lackawanna Valley, the University of Scranton was only two hours from where we lived, which allowed me ample opportunities to return home to my parents, who during this time had to face an empty house as all three of their children left them, one way or another, over the course of three years. This had to be hard for them. It was hard for all of us.

Chapter 10

THE BREAKDOWN

Attending college was a perfect getaway for me and a chance to start over and find some normalcy again. The liberal arts traditions of coursework it offered opened my eyes to the depth and breadth of human existence. In addition to the required science courses included with my major, I was exposed to the foundations of Plato's philosophy, explored the Bible as a historical document, contemplated the meaning of life and existence by reading Rollo May and Viktor Frankl, debated the principles of theology, struggled through Latin (thinking it would complement my courses in biology by assisting me with terminology—I was mistaken), read *Beowulf* and *The Canterbury Tales*, discussed the events of the Russian Revolution, and analyzed the great architecture in Art History. It was an exercise in intellectual gymnastics and forced me to rethink what I knew about the world. As much as I enjoyed these courses, it didn't take me long to realize I was ill-prepared for the academic demands of my major. Since most of my high school years centered around my brother's illness, the associated trauma and stress brought about by those experiences certainly affected my academic preparation. My grades suffered, my concentration was not optimal, and, more alarming, I was not motivated to get any help. Some would say this was just a typical freshman adjustment to college and it would work itself out. I didn't see it that way. I had never had this much trouble and doubt in my classes before. My lack of engagement in high school was coming back to plague me.

My grades that first year were average, not terrible, but not good enough to stay in the program. I was in survival mode. Biology classes, thankfully, were going well. Chemistry, quite frankly, presented the biggest challenge as the workload was daunting and my study skills were not up to the task. I didn't realize it then, but I was flirting with episodes of depression and anxiety. I managed to navigate through periods of high elation and abnormally questionable behavior (which for some college students may be typical, but that was not me) followed by episodes of brooding and malaise that kept me from pursuing a fully engaged college experience. To cope, I did what any college student does to head off the blues and get back in the game. So, where's the party?

I certainly attended my share of weekend gatherings and managed to balance my social life and my academic responsibilities well enough to stay just above average and just below the radar. However, I was simply existing, missing my brother, worrying about my parents and my sister, and maybe feeling guilty that I didn't do enough of anything to help anybody, including myself. I had plenty of questions. *What the hell is wrong with me? What am I doing here? Am I really cut out for this?* And as usual, I had no answers.

Over the holiday and seasonal breaks that broke up the college calendar, I would return home and often enjoy late-night discussions and movie nights with my father. Sometimes he would open up to me about how he was coping since my brother's death. I knew there were other challenges. They had to be carrying financial burdens. I wasn't sure how my parents' relationship was going, although everything appeared to be okay. But how could it be?

Certain things were not open to discussion. My father did, however, begin to discuss death and what it must be like. He had his own questions. He had recently bought a book that he felt would help him find some answers and maybe even affirm his belief that Timmy was really in a better place. The 1969 book *On Death and Dying* by Swiss American psychiatrist Elisabeth Kübler-Ross was a popular and fascinating explanation of a groundbreaking theory on death.[1] It helped introduce the general population to an analysis of the stages of grief and would lead to a movement to improve the way we care for the terminally ill. The Kübler-Ross model included five stages of grief: Denial, Anger, Bargaining, Depression, and Acceptance. Since this book was published, other theories have listed seven stages and even twelve stages of grief, but this was the first and most popular account.

My father read other books on near-death experiences as he not only wanted to know what he was going through but also what my brother may have experienced. This is about the time he started to question his faith. He could not understand how a loving and compassionate God could allow a child to suffer so much. It was a thought he carried with him for many years, and he even attempted to obtain some answers from the leaders of our faith.

Since St. Francis Church became a cathedral and the parish was christened as the Diocese of Metuchen, a new clerical patriarch was chosen to lead the flock. In 1981, Theodore McCarrick was named Bishop of Metuchen. Metuchen became relevant as a centerpiece of the Catholic faith in New Jersey with this high-profile appointment and a source of pride for the community. Upon his arrival, Bishop McCarrick asked the parishioners to anonymously submit questions to him that he would attempt to answer during religious services. Needing to pursue some comfort, Dad submitted his question: How could a loving and compassionate God allow children to suffer? This was an honest attempt to assuage his grief and find some explanation for the inexplicable. He was turning to those who might help him see the light.

During one Mass Bishop McCarrick surprisingly selected my father's question, read it aloud, and gave the congregation a rather stunning answer. He went on to proclaim that the suffering of children was due to the sins of their parents, and if the parents had followed the teachings of Christ, they may have been spared this pain. WHAT? Did he just blame the parents for their child's afflictions? My father was outraged! This was a typical "you are a sinner and are always a sinner" lecture from a church leader who apparently thought religious guilt was the way to keep a congregation faithful. *It's not God—it's you! You need to be punished for your sins and seek forgiveness, and good will come to you.* What a cold and heartless response. My father turned to the church for comfort and was summarily slapped down in public. Although these questions were anonymous, there were undoubtedly some churchgoers who could make the connection. This is not a big town. Dad *never* forgave the bishop for this.

After a few years, Bishop McCarrick moved on to become Archbishop of Newark, then held the same position in Washington, D.C., and it was there he was elevated to cardinal by Pope John Paul II in 2001. There was talk he was on a path to the papacy as a rising star for the Vatican. However, karma has a way of exercising its version of penance. The bishop became embroiled in a sickening scandal that was unfortunately becoming all too familiar to many Catholics. Repeated allegations involving the sexual abuse of teenage boys and seminarians came to light and made national headlines. This ultimately led to McCarrick's resignation from the College of Cardinals, and in 2019, he was defrocked by the Vatican.[2] He maintained his innocence through the years, but as he aged, he was ultimately deemed unfit for an upcoming trial due to a diagnosis of dementia, and a judge dismissed the case in August of 2023. I know my father did not have much sympathy for him, and this reinforced his feeling of the arrogance of power that undermines trust in our leaders. He knew he wasn't responsible for his son's illness, but it didn't make it any easier to have his faith called out so publicly.

We were all trying to cope in our own ways. Although we talked about Timmy quite often and with great affection and humor, we did not address what we were feeling and how we were coping. This was not a time when counseling was readily accessible or affordable. Unlike today, where counseling centers are available in virtually every community, trained personnel in every school, and in some cases, the costs are mitigated by insurance to improve access to mental health services, those options were not available or even considered at the time. Going to counseling had more of a stigma attached to it than it does today. You either dealt with it within the family or maybe even sought out your priest for spiritual guidance. But what if you questioned that spiritual guidance? Where do you go and who do you talk to? There was no way I was going to burden my parents with my problems after what they had been through.

So, sidestepping the real issue, my father and I talked about the Kübler-Ross book, and the discussions added to my understanding and to my confusion as I struggled with my feelings. Reading about the five stages, I didn't see how they fit since

I never felt I was in denial and didn't understand bargaining. Apparently, I skipped the preliminaries and began to develop a certain kinship with anger and depression.

In April of my sophomore year in college, it was coming up to the fourth anniversary of my brother's passing. Due to school being in session, I was not able to be home with my parents, who had a memorial Mass said for him each year at the cathedral. This was a difficult time for them, and for the first time, I was not there to lend support, which bred more frustration and anger.

One Saturday night, after yet another party and a few more beers than normal and not feeling much in the partying mood, I returned early to my room, which was in an off-campus apartment building. I felt an immense amount of guilt, and, completely unable to rein in my emotions, it just all came out. I exploded in a rage that I had never felt before. I had always been a bit high-strung, but this was a full-blown emotional eruption. The last six years of painful thoughts, unanswered questions, failed hopes, shattered dreams, death, suffering, all of it was unleashed. I threw anything that wasn't nailed down—chairs, cans, books, and desks—in a furious attempt to destroy anything and everything I could get my hands on as if this tirade would make it all go away. I screamed, cried, cursed God, cursed everyone and everything. I was unloading all that I had held back in a feeble attempt to exorcise these demons. Maybe by breaking everything I could repair myself.

All this time I had to stay strong for my parents, my sister, and my community, but I wasn't strong. I was collapsing under the weight of guilt, not being able to help, not understanding what was happening, not getting answers, not living up to my academic responsibilities and expectations, and the realization that I had no plan and no purpose. That night, it all just came out, and I couldn't control it. I was done holding back.

The room was trashed! Thankfully, no one in the small building was around to witness this meltdown, except for my roommate, Don. He happened to come in midway through this outburst and, though alarmed and concerned, allowed me to get it out of my system. When it was over and I had finally exhausted myself, he sat down with me and talked me through it. He knew my past, since as roommates for the past two years, we shared our experiences as we got to know each other. He knew me and he showed amazing patience and compassion. He kept this between us. We put the room or what was left of it back together and never spoke about it again. I will always be grateful to him for his kindness that night.

This breakdown, as I saw it, was another in a series of moments that ended one phase of life and initiated the next. After that night, for some reason, I felt a little more together despite falling apart. I was embarrassed but I was also relieved. Like everything else, I would try to analyze it to make some sense of this irrationality. Maybe it had to happen. Without the proper counseling, I was left to deal with my grief and guilt on my own, and I did a lousy job of it. I needed a purpose and a plan because this was an unacceptable way to live.

I began to rethink my academic path and converted my major to Biology Education, where I would continue to enjoy my chosen course of study while pursuing a possible career in the field of education. I had not seriously entertained the thought of being a teacher before this, but it was clear that a career in medicine or health care was not in the cards. It became a more comfortable thought. There were teachers throughout my family history, so maybe this was part of my DNA. So, I embraced it. For some odd and unknown reason, this breakdown led to a sense of clarity, a release of suppressed emotions that kept me from functioning at a high level. Timmy's Wish was an exclamation of purpose and a call to service, a lesson in humility and an answer to a higher calling. Same goal, different paths. Timmy sought his purpose in the church. I searched for mine in the classroom.

When I began my required student teaching experience at Scranton Central High School during my senior year, it all started to make sense. From the moment I entered the classroom, I had a feeling that this was what I was looking for and what I needed. Admittedly, I was not very good at first. Poorly planned lab demonstrations, organizational issues, and a broken projector later, I began to find my way with the support and patience of a terrific group of students who allowed me to fail with dignity while giving their best every day. The support they provided made the long daily walk from my apartment to the school in subfreezing temperatures eminently bearable. Though I did not realize it at the time, I was beginning to understand Timmy's Wish more each day.

Chapter 11

A DAY AT THE BEACH

My sister graduated college and then immediately set off to begin her nursing career at Tufts New England Medical Center in Boston. Her career was ascendant, moving from nursing to management. Her responsibilities grew with each new step, and she was as successful as I wished I could be. I don't know how she coped with it all. We never talked about it and, as with my parents, I would never bring it up. She seemed to have it together, but I am sure she had her moments and I know she felt guilty being so far away. She was much better at talking to my parents, especially my mother. They had a different relationship. I know my mother desperately missed her, and I was not much help because I was not one for talking and sharing or being empathetic. I just didn't know how and, unfortunately, didn't try very hard. Coleen was good at this. I was too focused on myself. This bothered my mother, and she occasionally reminded me that I didn't live in the house alone. All she wanted to know was how was my day going, and I left her with a dismissive, one-word answer, "fine."

I graduated college, returned home, and went about my business, constantly assuring the family everything was okay, but still not sharing. Timmy was not far from our thoughts. His

"Wish" still hung from the dining room wall, and I often walked by, stopping to read it repeatedly, still in awe that a fourth grader could write something so profound. But now it had a different meaning. There was a lesson here somewhere. What was he trying to say?

My first teaching job was at St. Peter's Catholic High School in New Brunswick, New Jersey, a short fifteen-minute ride from home. It didn't pay much, but it was a job and a start. Standing in front of a classroom of students, I realized my role in their educational experience and their future was an enormous responsibility, but I embraced it.

One of my colleagues at this distinctly religious institution told me after I arrived, "You're doing God's work, so do it well." I chuckled slightly at her enthusiasm, because growing up Catholic I understood the sentiment that we were a community of service. We teach to instruct, inspire, and point the way to a productive and fulfilling life. Okay! Sounds good. But my job was to teach Biology classes, and I looked forward to sharing my interest with my students. Being just an okay Catholic, I wasn't looking to save any souls. I would leave that to the professionals.

My students at St. Peter's High were just what I needed at the start of my career. They were not much younger than I was at that time and about the same age as my brother had he still been with us. Because of that, I was developing a sort of big brother complex where I felt especially responsible for their well-being and education. I worked very hard to be the best teacher I could. This was the first time where selfish thoughts were pushed aside and my energies directed toward others. Their hope and dreams, their problems and insecurities were very familiar territory, and I felt I could be of value to them as an instructor and a mentor. And I could do all of this and still teach biology? This could be fun. It was my job, my responsibility, and to be honest, my therapy. My high school experience was less than memorable, but watching the students navigate their journey, I could see how it was supposed to be.

In addition, I was offered a position as an assistant boys basketball coach, and everything started to fall in place. Through coaching and teaching, I was beginning to finally find my way. I gave my players and my students, my best effort, and they returned the favor. They were amazing young people. Bright, funny, hardworking, they trusted me with their education. That was more than I deserved.

However, after three years it was time to try the public school circuit because, quite frankly, I needed to make more money. Although I was "doing God's work," he wasn't going to pay the bills.

After leaving St. Pete's I had difficulty landing another teaching job in high schools. Multiple interviews yielded few offers of any significance. I had gained confidence over the last three years, so that was not the issue. There had to be a place out there for me to apply my skills.

It was mid-August, and I was still unemployed. Throughout the long summer of futile attempts to land a position, I would occasionally whisper to myself, "Hey, Tim, a little help here! Not asking for much, but if there is something you can do, I would certainly appreciate it." My prior experiences with hope and prayers did not go well, so I didn't expect much, but it couldn't hurt.

Shortly afterward, I received a phone call from my aunt at Georgian Court College. She heard from a colleague that a small elementary school down the Jersey Shore was looking for a middle school science teacher to fill in for a maternity leave vacancy. I was not particularly interested in teaching middle school as I was a high school teacher, so it was not a consideration at the time. I also felt, and wrongly so, this would be a step down and delay getting me back to where I was most familiar. It was also only a temporary one-year position, and that was not attractive either. I told my aunt that it was not what I was looking for and politely declined and thanked her for the information. Almost the next day the principal of the school called me (how did she get our number?) and asked if I would be interested in interviewing for the vacancy. I thought that was odd considering I didn't even apply for the job. It was getting late in the summer, and she seemed somewhat desperate, but then again so was I. Reluctantly and with no expectations, I agreed to take the ride down the shore and see what this was all about. And if it was a bust, it was still a day at the beach! So why not?

Some decisions you make—or don't make—change the course of your life in inconceivable ways. Little did I know that this meeting was going to change the trajectory of my life and my career.

I took the forty-minute ride down to Manasquan, a quaint and beautifully maintained borough along the Jersey Shore. I was a bit early for the interview, so I killed some time and drove around town to get a feel for the area. The elementary school sat on the western edge of town right across the street from the high school, giving it an interesting, campus-like feel. Main Street, which was lined with shops, a bakery, and a pharmacy, had a surprisingly familiar feel. Just east of the downtown area of Main Street there was, of course, a New Jersey Transit railroad line running north and south, splitting the town down the middle. There were churches of all denominations, including a large Catholic church just south of Main Street, residential homes within walking distance of all amenities, and further east, over the tracks, are you freakin' kidding me? A beach!

The summer was winding down, but the beach was bustling with activity. Bicycles lined up everywhere indicated the local kids just rode down the street to enjoy surfing, sand, and friends. This was amazing! This was Metuchen! With a beach! I had to make a point of visiting here someday.

I headed back to the school for my interview and was greeted by a very pleasant and professional secretary by the name of Fran Weeks, who took me into the office to meet with the principal, Liana Lang. The meeting lasted nearly an hour and included a tour of the building and an especially detailed look at the science lab, which was adequate for a middle school class with the typical lab tables, safety equipment, sinks, and gas outlets. The principal was making a hard sales pitch, and I thought, sarcastically, if this place was so good why couldn't they fill this position?

Despite my newly found interest in this town, I again politely declined the position for the same reason as before: I was a high school teacher. The principal looked at me and said, "I think you will be a good fit here." I said I would think about it. I went on my way and, yes, did give it some thought while I traveled north on the Garden State Parkway. I had a very unusual feeling. This place was different. It felt like I had been there before, even though I didn't quite remember stepping foot in this town. It was so much like Metuchen! And it had a beach!

My desperate request to my little brother looked more like an answer to a prayer. This was happening way too fast. If I didn't take this job, would there be another one waiting somewhere? Since this was late in the summer, time was running out. I knew this was an opportunity I could not decline. Even if it didn't work out, it was only for one year, so it would at least be an experience to put on my résumé.

The next day I contacted the principal and said I would accept the position. Having to move quickly we made plans for me to come down, meet the superintendent for final approval and then acceptance by the Board of Education at their next meeting. Done.

I couldn't help but look at Timmy's Wish, still hanging in the dining room, without wondering if he had something to do with this. I had heard everything about the saints, the miracles attributed to them, and how people's lives were changed because they believed in those miracles. A job is certainly not a miracle, but its impact on my life was just as profound! It was clear that this small town was a big deal.

Although I struggled adjusting to middle school teaching that first year, I was, as Mrs. Lang predicted, fitting in quite nicely. My students, although challenging as young teens can be, were amazing! There was so much energy, so much joy, and so much fun, mixed with a little bit of aggravation and irritation, but that just made it more interesting. I was adapting to new ways of teaching and growing as a person and a professional. Manasquan was the gift that kept on giving when in my second year (the maternity leave was extended) I secured a position as a basketball coach and met a young, incredibly talented student teacher named Cindy, who ultimately gained her own elementary teaching position in the same school. Not long after, we were planning our future together and our version of the American Dream. Oh, and that friendly professional secretary named Fran, who greeted me upon my initial arrival… she was Cindy's mother and my future mother-in-law. You can't make this up.

The hits just kept on coming. The principal eventually offered to keep me in that position permanently and reassigned the returning teacher to another grade level. She was showing her confidence in me, and I was determined to make the best of it. Over the years I continued to coach basketball and teach science, then transferred over to the high school to join the Science department, only this time better equipped and more experienced than the first time around. I attained my master's degree, from the familiar Georgian Court College, then transitioned into administration, where I spent twenty-three years as the assistant principal of the same elementary school where I started. After a total of thirty-six enormously rewarding years, I retired from this district where, ironically, I originally declined to accept a position.

In a tip of the cap and an homage to Mick Jagger, I paraphrase one of his lyrics, that sometimes in life you may not get what you want, but rather, you may get what you need. I may not have initially wanted Manasquan, but I needed Manasquan. It provided me with a life, a wife, and a purpose.

Living in the surrounding area, my two daughters, Sarah and Shannon, were fortunate to attend Manasquan High School and found success in academics and athletics. The friends and relationships we acquired over the years in this community were in stark contrast to an earlier time when I avoided such interactions. The difference between my two lives could not have been more distinct. It's as if everything that was lost was coming back tenfold. It seemed too good to be true. Timmy was certainly looking out for me.

Chapter 12

REUNITED

Looking back and reflecting on the totality of the events that led me to this point, I can only be grateful for being able to take these experiences and come away with an appreciation for life's opportunities, respect for life's challenges, and admiration for all who persevere through the most difficult times. The often-used phrase "Whatever doesn't kill you makes you stronger" meant nothing to me. It didn't make me stronger; it wrecked me. But I survived and so did my family. Battered and bruised we managed to climb out of a hole to find meaning in our lives. What I hope is that I am wiser, more empathetic, more appreciative due to this experience. Strength is not what I wanted. I wanted answers. Although answers still await somewhere in the ether of our existence, they are not essential at this time. That time will come. Timmy's legacy and his Wish gave me direction to find a purpose in my life. It was central to what we aspire to and believe.

In the years that followed my brother's death, my parents were able to return our lives to some form of normalcy, albeit a different kind of normal. I truly believe their agony was manifested in their declining physical health over the years. My mother suffered from the effects left over from the emotional trauma she experienced. She was a constant worrier. Her nerves were fried from those long, dark days in the hospital when it was just her and Timmy battling the tumor, the doctors, and the chemotherapy together. She felt every needle and lived through every grueling treatment. But she never lost her faith and knew they would one day be together again, only this time with no doctors, no chemo, no tears, no pain. I don't know what the criteria are for sainthood, but she qualifies in our opinion. Her decency and kindness are her legacy. Always thinking of others instead of herself, she was the living embodiment of her son's Wish.

Over time my mother developed breathing and cardiac issues—exacerbated, I'm sure, by a broken heart—that she quietly kept to herself until one October evening in 2010, when she collapsed from what we knew was a massive heart attack. She never knew what hit her. Shortly thereafter, as a family and in consultation with doctors, we made the difficult decision to remove her from life support. A day later she was gone. In some way, I think we were somewhat relieved that she didn't have to suffer a long demise. That would have been a cruel irony that was not necessary.

My father had his share of health issues. Stress certainly took its toll over the years as he heroically tried to keep the family together, trying to make decisions to save his son while keeping his head above the financial waters. He was also battling his faith. He never could reconcile how a loving and compassionate God could let a child suffer like that. Although he buckled, he didn't break. He came to find comfort in his faith and did not fear death because he believed in his son and that they would all be reunited sometime soon. He suffered years of challenging illnesses and numerous surgeries for cardiac disease, pacemakers, prostate cancer, skin cancer, stomach cancer, and a body riddled with osteoarthritis, all of which he stared down and nearly conquered. He was in constant pain, telling us the only time he felt pain-free was when he was lying down. He possessed a remarkable disposition toward this endless array of afflictions.

I once asked him how he dealt with the constant pain and maintained a sense of humor after all he had been through. Somewhat humored by my question, he said with a slight chuckle, delivered in a fading Brooklyn accent, "I just dismiss what I can't control. Whaddya gonna do—complain? Who's gonna listen anyway?" He prophetically continued with one of his more common locutions. "No one goes through life unscathed," he would say with his trademark smirk.

I was also curious as to how he navigated the severe financial difficulties this whole ordeal had caused. My sister and I continued to attend Catholic high school, found money for proms and class trips, and went to college in successive years, and this was immediately after the most challenging of times. Of course, both of us worked and contributed to our share of our expenses, but it certainly did not cover all the costs. Later in my father's life, when I had the chance, I asked him that question. He revealed to me some very surprising things that he thought were not necessary for us to know at the time.

Aside from taking out a second mortgage on the house, I was aware that he asked the monsignor of our parish church for some financial assistance; however, I do not know if that ever was realized or how much. He also revealed for the first time how our broken front steps were replaced. We had wooden steps leading to our front door that were in a state of disrepair, and one step was cracking and unsafe. My father was afraid someone would be injured, and he would be hit with a lawsuit, so it seems the neighbors got together and raised the money, not just to repair but to replace the wooden steps with a new and safer brick staircase with iron railings. This put my parents at ease knowing what could have happened if someone hurt themselves on their steps. My father was a very proud man but had to put that aside to humbly accept this charity under the current conditions.

This was not the only sign that our community had helped to keep us afloat. Due to tuition expenses at our Catholic high school, my parents had entertained the possibility of having to send us to the local public high school. This was not something my parents wanted to do or shared with us at the time. The money just wasn't there. However, an anonymous donor, a woman from the community, decided to pay the tuition for my sister's final year and my final two years of high school so that we could stay in the Catholic system. She knew all about my brother and our family and wanted to do her part. My father never determined the identity of this woman, but it was a gesture of great compassion and a demonstration of faith in us at a time when the help was greatly appreciated.

In addition, my parents received a substantial amount of money that accompanied sympathy cards and Mass cards. These were just a few of the many generous donations of time, money, meals, and other resources that our close-knit community provided to our family to help make our lives just a bit easier during difficult circumstances. My parents were overwhelmed with the support. I now understand why they were always available for friends, relatives, and others in the community and were very generous with their time and resources. This was how communities of faith support each other. I felt that Timmy's acts of compassion and generosity were well known in the community and provided the inspiration that led to this assistance. He always was and still is looking out for us. Another lesson from heaven.

My sister continued her very successful career path and eventually moved back to New Jersey with her husband, Dan Rossi, and her two sons, Timmy (named after my brother) and Kyle. After my mother passed, my sister offered to take my father into her home, where she had an extra room, and there, he would spend his final eight years. This was a time when he was able to see all four of his grandchildren more regularly. He enjoyed hearing about their school experiences and athletic accomplishments, proudly attended games and each graduation, and especially the sarcastic banter back and forth with my nephews, who dished it out just as well as the master. I told my sister that I truly believed being around the boys every day added years to my father's life.

Eventually, all the illnesses caught up to him. We made yet another difficult decision to put him in a nursing facility, and though he was not happy about it, he didn't want to be a burden to my sister and her family any longer, as his health required more and more specialized attention. The roles had flipped, and we were making difficult decisions for him. We agreed, with his blessing, to have a standing Do Not Resuscitate (DNR) order put in place and had his pacemaker disconnected so he wouldn't have to experience the shock of the pacemaker's defibrillator in his final hours. After a trying three months, his heart slowly and quietly lost the strength to maintain him, and he passed quietly in his sleep, somewhat coincidentally, just before the 100-day limit on what insurance would cover and he would have to draw down what was left of his modest financial resources. We found a little bit of humor and comfort in the irony of the moment. It's almost like he planned this. Just like him to have the final say! Hospitals took almost everything he had years ago, and he wasn't giving them another nickel.

One of the blessings that has come from this was that my sister and I were present at the moment when all three of them passed. None of them were alone in their final hours, as it should be. This was a gift for both of us to be able to be present at a time when they transitioned from this life to another free of pain and suffering.

My parents and Timmy, all three of them finally reunited after so many years apart. I often wonder if my father had the experience he read about in his books on death and dying. I never felt he feared death and maybe even looked forward to it in some way. He had the foresight to create a burial plot at Resurrection Cemetery that would accommodate all three of them. He relocated my brother's casket and placed him next to my mother. On the other side was a spot reserved for him when his time came. Timmy was right in the middle as it should be now and forever. The headstone is adorned with the family name, and just underneath is a subtle banner that reads:

We lived together in happiness, we rest together in peace.

Just below that and prominently displayed in its entirety just as it was on the dining room wall is **"MY WISH."** Perfect!

Chapter 13

THE WAY FORWARD

Timmy's Wish is a message of purpose, a lesson in humility, service, and enduring faith. In one short paragraph, he laid out a plan, a spiritual mission that transcends the physical world. He knew something and this was his way of expressing it. However, questions still haunt me as they do with anyone who loses a loved one, especially a child who, through no fault of their own, has been robbed of reaching their full potential and pursuit of a happy and productive life with their continued achievements and impacts remaining unknown. Who could he have been? What could Timmy have accomplished if given the chance? What if he did become a priest and was able to inspire his congregation to find their spiritual purpose? With the state of the world as it is, why are the angels taken to heaven when we need them here?

For those left to ponder the unanswerable and deal with picking up the pieces of broken dreams and shattered lives, it is the emotional challenges that present the greatest obstacle to returning to a fulfilling life. One reason why I shared my family's struggles in this book was to shed some light on the impact of what these incredibly disruptive events can have on a family that is thrown into a milieu of medical terminologies, decisions, and the consequences thereof, without any forewarning or preparation. One day everything seems just fine, and one diagnosis later your entire life is turned upside down as you attempt to process an event you do not understand that presents an outcome you can't possibly fathom. And yet, you are not alone.

Here are some sobering statistics. According to the American Childhood Cancer Organization (ACCO), each year, 15,780 children from birth to nineteen years of age will be diagnosed with cancer. Approximately one in 285 will be diagnosed before their twentieth birthday. Cancer remains the most common cause of death by disease for children.[1] Since 1975, the year of Timmy's passing, there has been an increase of an average of 0.8 percent per year in childhood cancer diagnoses, with the average age being ten years, according to Children's Cancer Cause (CCC).[2] This also means that 15,780 families are getting this news and having to cope with the unthinkable. The CCC goes on to state that the estimate of children diagnosed with cancer from 2020–2050 will be 13.7 million cases with 45 percent of them going undiagnosed, and if they do survive, 95 percent of those individuals will have significant health-related conditions by the time they reach forty-five years of age.

Medical research has come a long way since the 1970s, and most new cancer drugs are for the more common cancers in children: leukemia (28.1%) and brain/central nervous system (CNS) cancers (26.5%).[3]

Other modern techniques still include advanced chemotherapies in conjunction with surgery and radiation; however, research into bio adhesive nanoparticles that "stick" to the tumor and release molecules to disrupt the process that promotes tumor activity,[4] along with targeted therapy options, immunotherapy in combination with advanced imaging techniques, clinical trials, and personally targeted and supportive care are improving the options available. Today, the tumor that afflicted my brother, pilocytic astrocytoma, has a five-year survival rate of 97 percent for children under the age of fifteen.[5] Although there is always the fear of recurrences, the increased odds of survival, even in the short term, allow for more time as medical science moves forward in research and innovation.

Beyond direct medical intervention, there is a movement to improve supportive care for not only the patients but for the families. This is called palliative care. It is simply described as providing specialized medical care for the patient and supportive care for the families, which may include honest communication about treatment goals, consultation around the idea of continued care, shared decision-making, financial counseling, and grief or bereavement services. Palliative care differs from hospice in that hospice is comfort care without medical intervention for a cure. At that point, it is more end-of-life care.

Jennifer Cullen, PhD, MPH, a cancer epidemiologist, in her 2014 article "Because Statistics Don't Tell the Whole Story: A Comprehensive Care for Children with Cancer," written for the American Childhood Cancer Organization (ACCO), made an impassioned call to address "underfunded resources to upgrade childhood cancer treatment" and identified the need to assist with the lifelong challenges facing families of children who do not survive. In the article, she revealed that she had lost her daughter to cancer, and this experience gave her insight into the need for improved family care. She went on to state that "grief begins at diagnosis" and that childhood cancer is "a family disease" and should be treated with that in mind.[6]

Palliative care may even include assisting children who survive to transition back to school while still undergoing treatment or post-treatment care for ongoing side effects. Many cancer hospitals such as St. Jude, Memorial Sloan Kettering, and the

Dana Farber Institute, among others, offer comprehensive programs in palliative care. This is all light-years ahead of what was available in the 1970s.

Grief is an enduring emotion and a formidable adversary to one's emotional health, and it is important to understand the effects and the power of grief. Grief is a response to loss and carries with it many emotions that can be overwhelming. There is anger about a loss, a fear of what is to come, bitterness and regret at what could have been done or what could have been achieved. It also has significant effects on the body, leading to chronic stress and anxiety, physical pain, the suppression of immune responses, which help you to fight off illnesses, and can even rewire the brain, resulting in memory and cognitive issues. Grief can even affect the heart muscle, causing symptoms similar to a heart attack, such as chest pain, shortness of breath, arrhythmias, a weakening of the left ventricle of the heart, and heart palpitations. This has sometimes been referred to as "broken heart syndrome."[7] It may be temporary and reversible, but it is very real and could be triggered by sudden emotional responses to traumatic events. All these physiological responses should be brought to a physician to help properly manage these symptoms through therapies and possible use of medication if warranted.

Grief may also bring surprising benefits in a new appreciation and fondness for the life of a lost one, your own life, a sense of wisdom, and even greater motivation to find meaning in one's life. However, grief doesn't go away as much as it must be managed. It is important that anyone who experiences negative feelings while grieving needs to seek professional assistance to understand it and, more importantly, to learn to accept the situation at hand. There are many professional outlets in communities, hospitals, and even religious institutions that have trained counselors ready to assist in spiritual and self-care options. Acceptance brings with it a sense of healing, and grieving is a necessary part of that process. For years I fought grief, pretending it was something else, determined to deal with it on my own, and as a result found a breakdown waiting for me years after a traumatic event. It would have been worthwhile to know if there was help available; maybe some of my most challenging experiences could have been mitigated with some knowledge and skills to deal with them.

Anger mixed with episodes of depression were the obstacles I had to face without understanding what it was or how to deal with it. My parents did a good job of putting up a strong front for us, and it gave me an illusion that they were all right, and my sister and I should be also. But we weren't. However, we found comfort in our faith in God and our belief that this was not an end but a beginning of something greater for us as individuals and as a family both here on earth and beyond as we moved through to the acceptance of our past and were blessed by the lessons of Timmy's Wish.

Acceptance has allowed me to reflect on just how fortunate we were to have Timmy in our lives even for a short time. I have learned to appreciate the reality of life's challenges and face them, not retreat from them or ignore them. Acceptance, I hope, has made me a better husband, father, teacher, and coach. Acceptance has also led me to a greater appreciation for how lucky I am to have lived my life, so far, without affliction and pain, and I hope that continues for as long as possible. I have also gained the ability to see the good in people whom I used to doubt and suspect. The level of generosity that ordinary people engage in each day along with the immediate surge in care and support during catastrophic events—whether they be fires, floods, or national tragedies such as 9/11—is a testament to a society and a national culture that see the big picture and believe you are part of a greater good and answer to a higher power. Hints of that higher power are presented to us in our individual lives if we are willing to see it and accept it.

Whether or not Elisabeth Kübler-Ross was correct in her five stages of grief, I cannot be sure. Ultimately that is not important for our purposes here. That task belongs in the realm of the researchers from the relevant disciplines to tackle. However, she did understand the journey of those who faced loss when she made this insightful commentary from her 1975 book: *Death: The Final Stage of Growth:*

The most beautiful people we have known are those who have known defeat, known suffering, known struggle, known loss, and have found their way out of the depths. These persons have an appreciation, a sensitivity, and an understanding of life that fills them with compassion, gentleness, and a deep loving concern. Beautiful people do not just happen.[8]

Chapter 14

HEALING INVOLVES ACTION

Many families who have been through trauma are the silent heroes who have used their circumstances, their grief, and their newfound strength of purpose to find ways to alleviate the suffering of other families in similar circumstances to provide a community of support. There is nothing more powerful than a group or community organization that understands their plight and can guide them through their pain and put them in a better position to find the way to a meaningful existence. This support is so powerful and so necessary.

There are many organizations, local and national, that are dedicated to this mission. Whether it be to find resources for cures, financial support for families, or emotional support for those who are in the grips of a very powerful grief, they exist under many categories and are active in both public and private ventures. I would like to focus on the area I am personally familiar with, and that is pediatric cancer. This is also an area that provokes certain emotions because this affliction is not necessarily a sudden or dramatic, instantaneous event. It is more of a long-drawn-out series of actions and experimentation, testing and treatments, the roller coaster of elevated hopes and crushing disappointments. Families may undergo this struggle for years or even decades, sapping nearly all their personal resources and taking an enormous toll on the physical and emotional health of those directly involved. The goal is always patient survival, and even then, what is the future of their normal? Since we are dealing with children, the overwhelming feeling of unfairness at the injustice of it all adds to the burden, as they are our most innocent and vulnerable members of society.

Support comes from many sources. I will list some of the more well-known institutions here that could be points of contact for families of patients and a good place to start. This is by no means a complete list and is not meant to be. It is just a sampling of what may be available to you. I have no affiliation with or financial interest in any of these major organizations.

In my research for this book, I have been impressed with the number of options available today for families and the network of support and sponsorship they engage in to provide care and services. However, I would strongly advise anyone with an interest in volunteering or donating to any group or organization to do your homework on the types of services they offer, their financial distribution, the percentage of funds that go directly to the cause they champion, their sponsors, and their leadership structure. Make sure you are comfortable that they reflect your values, your needs or your vision. There are so many others in all states of our country that could be mentioned, but that would require another book. Check out the great work being done in your state in cancer research and treatment for children.

First are the medical facilities and research hospitals that provide medical care for pediatric cancer patients but have also developed programs for palliative care to offer comprehensive services for patients and families. Those listed below are ranked by U.S. News and World Report Health as some of the top pediatric cancer centers in the country for 2023–2024.[1] In no particular order they are:

NATIONAL AND REGIONAL

- St. Jude Research Hospital in Memphis, Tennessee. (www.stjude.org) For the rest of his life, despite modest resources, my father donated regularly to St. Jude with the hope that other families would not have to go through the experience we did.
- John Theurer Cancer Center in Hackensack, New Jersey (www.hackensackmeridian.org)
- The Dana Farber Cancer Institute in Boston, Massachusetts (www.danafarberbostonchildrens.org)
- Memorial Sloan Kettering Cancer Center in New York City, New York, and New Jersey (www.mskcc.org)
- Cincinnati Children's Hospital Medical Center in Cincinnati, Ohio (www.cincinnatichidrens.org)
- Children's Hospital in Los Angeles, California (www.chla.org)
- Texas Children's Hospital in Houston, Texas (www.texaschildren.org)
- Children's Hospital of Philadelphia (CHOP) Philadelphia, Pennsylvania (www.chop.edu)
- Johns Hopkins Children's Center in Baltimore, Maryland (www.hopkinsmedicine.org)
- Children's Healthcare of Atlanta, Georgia (www.choa.org)
- Children's National Hospital in Washington, D.C. (www.childrensnational.org)

- Children's Hospital Colorado in Aurora, Colorado (www.childrenscolorado.org)
- Mayo Clinic in Rochester, New York (www.mayoclinic.org)

New York/New Jersey Metro Area (also well respected)
- New York Presbyterian Children's Hospital in New York, New York (www.nyp.org)
- Cohen Children's Medical Center in Queens, New York (www.childrenshospital.northwell.edu)
- Mount Sinai Kravis Children's Hospital in New York, New York (www.mountsinai.org)
- Childrens Hospital at Montefiore Bronx, New York (www.cham.org)
- Hassenfeld Children's Hospital at NYU Langone in New York, New York (www.nyulangone.org)
- Rutgers Cancer Institute of New Jersey in New Brunswick, New Jersey (www.rwjbh.org)

Local (In my backyard, and well respected)
- K Hovnanian Children's Hospital at Jersey Shore University Medical Center in Neptune, New Jersey (www.hackensackmeridianhealth.org)
- Statesir Cancer Center at CentraState Cancer Hospital in Freehold, New Jersey (www.centrastaecancercenter.com)
- RWJ Barnabas Health Monmouth Medical Center in Long Branch, New Jersey (www.rwjbh.org)

FUNDRAISING AND SERVICE ORGANIZATIONS AND FOUNDATIONS

The following are just a few of the more well-known national or grassroots organizations that work privately or in affiliation with hospitals or medical centers to offer care and services to families of pediatric cancer patients while raising money to fund research. There are too many to mention, but this is a good start for anyone interested in getting more information.

- Alex's Lemonade Stand (www.alexslemonade.org)
- Cure Children's Cancer Charities (www.childhoodcancer.org)
- The V Foundation (www.v.org)
- The National Pediatric Cancer Research Foundation (www.pcrf-kids.org)
- National Children's Cancer SocietY (www.theccs.org)
- American Childhood Cancer Organization (www.acco.org)
- Leukemia and Lymphoma Society (www.lls.org)
- Children's Cancer Cause (www.children'scancercause.org)
- Cancer Research Institute (www.cancerresearch.org)
- Ronald McDonald Charities (www.rmhc.org)
- The Valerie Fund (www.thevaleriefund.org)
- American Cancer Society (www.cancer.org)
- Run With Veronica Foundation (www.runwithveronica.org)

Shout Out – I would like to proudly mention a local non-profit grassroots organization affiliated with my local school district in Manasquan, New Jersey. Manasquan High School sponsors the annual fundraising event called **Squan-A-Thon**, which annually raises money for families of children with pediatric cancer and other illnesses. It is a twelve-hour marathon of activities, music, speakers, and dancers that involves an impressive number of the student body who volunteer their efforts to this cause. It is modeled after the well-known Penn State THON at Penn State University (www.bjc.psu.edu) and relies primarily on individual or small business donations. It was originally brought to Manasquan by my former colleague Paul Battaglia, a teacher and Penn State graduate, and has grown into one of the most popular and incredibly successful annual school-based charitable events in New Jersey, consistently setting new fundraising records. I am proud that both of my daughters participated in this outstanding event for multiple years and have cited this as one of their fondest memories from high school. The website references fundraising efforts that have contributed to financial and emotional support to local families impacted by pediatric cancer and other serious illnesses. If you are interested in more information or wish to donate, visit their website www.squan-a-thon.org.

Grief Counseling

For those seeking information on grief counseling for themselves, their family members, or friends, there are a variety of online national and state counseling organizations that provide grief and bereavement services. Most local communities either have or are within a short distance of grief and counseling centers that provide services if you prefer a more in-person experience. Many K-12 public school districts, along with colleges and universities, have developed crisis teams that respond to assist their students and families. The social workers and school psychologists are well informed about the local counseling centers and even bring those individuals into the school to speak with students. Schools will also have information related to services in local hospitals that have emergency crisis interventions.

Regardless of how you go about seeking help, the important thing is that you *are* seeking help if you need it. Do not try to power through if you know there is a problem. There is an abundance of resources available, and the stigma of mental health counseling has decreased as the services and the awareness of the need for such have grown. Your life goes on. *You have a purpose!* Maintaining a healthy, grateful, and guilt-free existence will go a long way toward realizing your purpose and contribute to an inner resilience to face the challenges of life.

FOR EDUCATORS

If you are a teacher at any level in the educational system, you must get to know your students and, if possible, especially with younger students, their families. These relationships are vital to children who may be dealing with adverse situations that can affect their learning. When a child faces the loss of a loved one, especially one in their immediate family, it can result in reduced concentration, learning loss, and reduced student engagement.[2] Sometimes they may seem just fine. Smiling, laughing, and socializing are good indicators of coping but may also prevent a teacher from noticing any behaviors that could suggest deeper problems. If you have information about what your student has been through, yet they say they are okay, they still may not be okay. It is wise for the school to monitor their behavioral and academic progress as they go through a grieving process.

Neuroscience tells us what stress and anxiety do to a student's ability to learn. Although it is a complicated physiological process, it can be summarized to make the point. The brain is wired for awareness and survival, which is a good thing as a defense strategy. In short, when we are relaxed and feel safe, our brains can process information through our prefrontal cortex, which is involved in thinking and planning, and the information is consolidated in other parts of the brain, such as the hypothalamus, and relayed to processing and memory centers. When the brain is stressed or feeling extreme anxiety, this pathway is interrupted as the brain goes into a sort of survival mode where the amygdala, a small almond-shaped tissue in the center of the brain that is part of our "emotional brain," becomes activated to alert us to a fight-or-flight response (Dennis-Tiwary 2022).[3] In other words, when under stress, the brain is tied up performing other functions instead of focusing on learning.

School should not be another burden for the grieving child. Teachers with knowledge of a child's circumstances can be a source of empathy and compassion for the student as they incorporate strategies that can help calm anxiety and assist students in being more productive. Many schools are now developing *mindfulness* programs that teach skills that promote "an intentional focus of one's attention on the present moment in a nonjudgmental way" (Armstrong, 2019). These practices may also be combined with other behavioral models such as Social Emotional Learning (SEL) or Positive Behavioral Interventions and Support (PBIS), which, if used judiciously, can be integrated into an instructional plan in subtle but effective ways without taking away from the lessons of the general curriculum.[4]

As I have mentioned previously, these programs were not available during my time in school. My generalized "brain fog" that accompanied my high school experience may have negatively affected my ability to perform academically up to my potential, and it may have had consequences going forward. In fact, I am sure of it. Even as a teacher, I had students in class facing similar circumstances, but I did not have the training to assist them at the time nor did we have the services available in schools earlier in my career.

Today teachers, guidance counselors, social workers, and other staff are trained in how one can integrate some of these models into an instructional plan and a classroom culture to create a climate where a child can succeed. However, it is not recommended that classroom teachers take it upon themselves to counsel students in adverse mental states. There are professionals who are specifically trained and certified for just that purpose. Defer to them.

A teacher can be the first person a child confides in. A teacher can be one of the most important people in a child's life and even more so if they lose a parent or some other loved one. Empathy, compassion, understanding, and providing hope can go a long way to help children navigate their emotional swings along with knowing where to seek additional resources.

For Individuals – What Can You Do?

We are generous and caring people who recognize that what happens to anyone can happen to any of us. There but for the grace of God...as many say. The strengths of our communities are in the families, the friends, and the neighbors you grow up with, live next door to, or work with, and share the experiences of everyday life. They are in a unique position to provide personal and meaningful support to a grieving family because there is already a bond and sense of trust established because of those experiences. Those who have a personal relationship with the family or a family member are better suited to determining what is needed in the short and the long term.

Many communities come together and utilize crowd-sourcing apps to raise funds, gift cards, meals and meal vouchers, home maintenance, shopping services, and may even assist in setting up foundations to support a cause in memory of a loved one. These efforts can go a long way to ease the pressure of time and the stresses of financial obligations.

There are also ways an individual can help that require no monetary cost but may even be more impactful. Money can buy things, but things don't heal a soul. Emotional and spiritual support is very important throughout the grieving process. Even if someone is accessing professional services, having a close friend, neighbor, or valued member of the extended family available on a regular basis is enormously important. The best thing you can do is to be there. Your presence is your gift.

Not everyone may feel comfortable getting involved directly for fear of not knowing what to say or imposing upon a person who is going through a difficult time in their life. "Being emotionally supportive is not a natural skill for some but it is a skill that can be learned" (Legg, 2021).[5] With that in mind, there are simple ways to move your intentions into action. Some key features of emotional support are to:

Ask "How can I help you?" The grieving person may provide information that will help you to better help them.

Listen – Give them a space to talk. Be willing to sit in silence. They need to verbalize even if they do not want you to do anything. Just listening provides great comfort.

Validate their feelings. The feelings are real.

Offer Reassurance – There is hope. Hope always helps. Avoid offering advice during this time unless it is specifically requested.

Offer Encouragement – Build them up and highlight their strengths to help improve their resilience.

Check in Regularly – You will gain their trust through your dependability. Remember, grieving doesn't go away. It must be managed. Nobody wants to be alone. Loneliness and isolation breed anxiety and depression and have factored into increased risk for heart disease, stroke, diabetes, and earlier death.[6]

Physical Affection – A squeeze of a hand, a shoulder to cry on, or a consoling hug. Nothing feels better than a reassuring embrace from a close friend or family member. Without saying anything it conveys your support, your empathy, and that you will be there for them.[7]

Spiritual Support – A variety of spiritual resources for each faith is available in communities or online, either through private organizations or religious institutions. Help friends to seek out these resources, attend services with them, or just pray with them. Sharing your faith reminds them that they are part of a community that values the greater purpose and expectation of greater rewards in the next life. This can be very comforting. Don't underestimate the power of prayer and the long-term benefits of a deep and enduring faith. An important study has shown that spiritual belief may assist in resolving grief more rapidly with lower rates of recurrences.[8] I can attest to the fact that our faith as a family was a significant factor in our healing and continues to bring us comfort to this day.

Chapter 15

EPILOGUE

Timmy's Wish—written by a nine-year-old boy as an instinctive reflection of a school writing prompt—is a profound statement of recognizing one's purpose in life. I often wondered if it was a manifestation of divine inspiration or a faithful proclamation of a boy who had an extraordinary gift to visualize his existence beyond the ordinary, one where he would play a central role in a community of faith. What did he understand at such a young age that we do not despite our years that claim to bring us that wisdom? What makes this even more remarkable is that it would have been understandable if he wished to be a priest with an earthly purpose serving his congregation. But he didn't. He wished for more. He wished to be an institution, an idea, not a person or a structure. He saw his role beyond this world as a guide for those who sought a purpose to their existence and answers to their fundamental questions. He seemed to comprehend at some subconscious level that his place was not ultimately with us but in a state where he could serve the most souls. This is an uncommon thought for a young person and an extraordinary leap of consciousness that continues to amaze me and reminds us that maybe angels do exist all around us if we are willing to believe in the mission and the Wish.

For the rest of us, his Wish is a lesson in reflection and a motivation to think bigger and bolder while piecing together a meaningful life. Unfortunately, today self-reflection, self-improvement, and self-actualization trend more toward self-admiration for purposes of branding, monetization, or acceptance with the assistance of new technologies under the sometimes well-intentioned guise of influencing. This can result in a missed opportunity to deeply impact and inspire others to a degree that is personal and transformational. It would be more effective to have learned our lessons from those whose humility, simplicity, and wisdom elevate us to a broader more external view of our importance. A more meaningful importance. These lessons have been shared with us all along, provided by those who already know us, who have always seen our unlimited potential and challenged us to do more and be more if we are willing to listen, whether they are lessons from life or lessons from heaven.

Timmy wrote his Wish just a few months before his diagnosis. Did he know his time with us was limited? Was this his way of preparing us for the hard lessons ahead? Was he giving us hope that despite the difficulties that lay before us, we would be rewarded in the end if we kept our faith and followed his guidance? Whatever the reason his Wish is tangible evidence of his legacy and an example of how simple acts of humility and compassion can impact the lives of others in profound and consequential ways.

This was not an easy book to write. It has taken me several years to work up the courage to organize my thoughts to return to my past and acknowledge my failures in responding to and coping with such a disruptive life event. Timmy's loss was the most important and influential episode in my life and, I am sure, in the lives of my family.

As the years pass, maturity brings the realization that loss is part of life and grieving is part of the healing process. However, at the time I was only fifteen years old, and it was challenging enough to navigate the confusion and emotional restlessness of adolescence while then having to face a significant life-changing event without the necessary information and coping strategies. The effects led to years of anger, distrust, and doubt. I had many questions, and few of those were ever answered at the time. When looking for clarity from the institutions I grew up with, the results were less than satisfying. It would have been helpful for myself and my family to have been aware of and have access to any professional assistance that may have lessened the impact.

But we did have our faith. And while I questioned that faith from time to time when I was young, it eventually provided the needed comfort and understanding that there was some good to come from all this misery. Having a strong faith leads to a level of contentment, knowing that you do matter, your actions matter, and you can be a positive influence in a uniquely individual way. I am truly grateful for Timmy's inspiration in that I needed to find a purpose in my life, and his Wish was the motivation for that search. He taught me that we live for a higher commitment, and it centers around serving others. I found my purpose in the relationships with my family, my friends, and in the lives and experiences of each student I was, and still am, privileged to serve through the profession of teaching. Being an educator allowed me the opportunity to have a positive impact on students, but along the way, I found that it is their impact on me that became the difference, and I will be forever grateful to them.

I have so much respect for the way my parents and my sister handled this enormous burden. They never saw themselves as victims but recognized that life's cruelties do not discriminate, that there are many others whose burdens may even be greater, and that there are harsh realities that are more than offset by the joys of living a faithful life. They remain an inspiration.

Timmy was a remarkably gifted individual whose legacy in his community stands as a testament to his courage and his faith. Through his actions, he practiced what was preached and developed a statement of purpose—a mission statement for his life and a roadmap for us. My father was right. Timmy's story needed to be told. Timmy's Wish needed to be shared.

CHAPTER NOTES

CHAPTER 4

An interesting side note. Dr. Shulman died in 1981 at the age of 52 of "an apparent suicide." When our family found out about this, our thoughts focused on this highly respected doctor and the field he had chosen. We did not know the details, but we did consider whether a career in such a challenging vocation and the routine sadness and death that came with it could have been a contributing factor to his mental health. Cancer affects more than just the patient. https://nytimes.com/1981/03/24/obituaries/dr-kenneth-shulman

University of California San Francisco Brain Tumor Center. Pilocytic Astrocytoma Grade 1. https://braintumorcenter.ucf.edu/condition/pilocyticastrocytoma-grade retrieved October 2023.

Girardi, Fabio MD; Allemani, Claudia, PhD; Coleman, Michael FFPH. "Global Trends in Survival from Astrocytic Tumors in Adolescence and Young Adults: A Systematic Review." June 2020. ncbi.nlm.gov/pmc/articles/PMC7583144 retrieved October 2023.

4. See number 1.

CHAPTER 7

https://www.inquirer.com/philly/obituaries/20111114_Isaac_Djerassi_86_physican_who_advanced_cancer_therapy.html retrieved October 2023.

CHAPTER 10

Kubler-Ross, Elisabeth, Dr. On Death and Dying: What the Dying Have to Teach Doctors, Nurses, Clergy, and Their Own Families. 1969 Macmillan Publishing Co.

"Ex-Cardinal McCarrick Not Competent to Stand Trial in Abuse Case Brought by NJ Accuser." Associated Press NorthJersey.com. Aug. 30, 2023 retrieved October 2023.

CHAPTER 13

"Childhood Cancer Statistics." American Childhood Cancer Statistics https://www.acco.org-cancer-statistics/ retrieved October 2023.

"Children's Cancer Facts." https://www.childrenscancer-cause.org/facts retrieved October 2023.

Ibid.

Weir, William. "New Treatment Merges Two Technologies to Fight Brain Cancer." Feb 2023. news.yale.edu/2023/02/08 retrieved October 2023.

"Astrocytoma Childhood Statistics." https://www.cancer.net retrieved October 2023.

Cullen, Jennifer PhD. "Because Statistics Don't Tell the Whole Story: A Comprehensive Care for Children with Cancer." MPH 2014 American Childhood Cancer Organization https://acco.org retrieved October 2023.

"Broken Heart Syndrome." https://www.myclevelandclinic.

org/brokenheartsyndrome retrieved October 2023.

Kubler-Ross, Elisabeth, Dr. Death: The Final Stage of Growth. 1975 Prentice-Hall.

CHAPTER 14

"Best Children's Hospitals for Cancer." US News Health. https://health.usnews.com/cancer retrieved October 2023.

Schonfield, David, MD. "Grieving Children: An Essential Role for Schools." https://www.etr.org retrieved October 2023.

Dennis-Tiwary, Tracey, PhD. Future Tense: Why Anxiety Is Good for You (Even Though It Feels Bad). 2022. HarperCollins Publisher. New York, New York. pg. 35.

Armstrong, Thomas. Mindfulness in the Classroom: Strategies for Promoting Concentration, Compassion, and Calm. ASCD Alexandria, Virginia, 2019. pg. 19.

Legg, Timothy J. PhD. "How to Be Emotionally Supportive." September 2021. https://www.healthline.com retrieved October 2023.

"Health Risks of Social Isolation and Loneliness." https://cdc.gov retrieved October 2023.

"Helping Someone Who Is Grieving." https://helpguide.org retrieved October 2023.

Walsh, Kiri; King, Michael; Tookman, Adrian; Blizard, Robert. "Spiritual Beliefs May Affect Outcomes of Bereavement: Prospective Study." PMC. National Library of Medicine National Center for Biotechnology Medicine. June 2002. https://ncbi.nlm.nih.gov retrieved October 2023.

ACKNOWLEDGMENTS

Inspiration comes in many forms and my eternal gratitude goes to the many doctors, nurses and other health care professionals who dedicate their lives to helping families through some of most difficult challenges they will face. They are heroes.

To the many students and student athletes, past and present, that I have taught or coached, who continue to inspire me and remind me daily of the simple joys of teaching, learning, and competing.

To all the teachers who understand the power and gift of the classroom. You are doing God's work.

To my parents for their lessons of strength, faith, and family. They set the foundation for us to build on. I pray they found the peace they deserve.

To my sister Coleen Rossi, for her contributions to this book and never-ending support. You have always been there for us and it's a comfort to know you always will be.

To Timmy who continues to teach and guide me. His life is a lesson, his Wish is his legacy.

To my daughters, Sarah and Shannon, who remind me every day how blessed I am.

To my wife, Cynthia, for your constant love, support and understanding. You make it all possible.

Printed in the USA
CPSIA information can be obtained
at www.ICGtesting.com
CBHW030601110524
8411CB00007B/131